WE BLAZED THE TRAIL

First published in 2008 by

WOODFIELD PUBLISHING LTD
Bognor Regis ~ West Sussex ~ England ~ PO21 5EL
www.woodfieldpublishing.com

ISBN 1-84683-049-4

We Blazed the Trail

An illustrated history of the

Civil Defence Experimental Mobile Column 1953/4

COMPILED BY

ROBIN G. REID &

MALCOLM BIDDER

Woodfield

Woodfield Publishing Ltd

Woodfield House ~ Babsham Lane ~ Bognor Regis ~ West Sussex ~ PO21 5EL

telephone 01243 821234 ~ **e-mail** enquiries@woodfieldpublishing.com

Interesting and informative books on a variety of subjects

For full details of all our published titles, visit our website at

www.woodfieldpublishing.com

We dedicate this book to
all our former EMC comrades

Photo 1. EMC shoulder flash.

Photo 2. Robin G. Reid and Malcolm Bidder

Photo 3. Commemorative plaque on the wall of Sainsbury's supermarket at Kiln Lane, Epsom, which now stands on the site of the former Mobile Column training ground.

~ CONTENTS ~

Photo 4. A few news clippings about the EMC.

Preface

It was February 1955 and I was being demobbed from Tofanau in North Wales. Curly White and I went hurtling down to Tofanau railway station, which was like a request stop, if nobody was there the train carried on, so there was no time to lose.

Curly and I had been mates since our time together in the EMC at Epsom in 1954 and here we were, ready to say our goodbyes but promising to keep in touch…

Back in civvy street I found a job and continued to court my girlfriend, who I'd met whilst serving in Epsom, some 50 miles away from my home town of Chesham in Buckinghamshire. Thankfully, it didn't take me long at the weekend to visit, as I had an Excelsior Manxman motorbike, which went like a rocket!

In the same year I married and we moved to Ashtead in Surrey, where we lived until 1957, when we started a family and decided to move to my home town of Chesham, where the years rolled by, but in spite of my always remembering the promise Curly and I had made, to keep in touch, somehow I never got round to it.

When I retired, my wife was clearing away decades-worth of things we might have used but never did, when she came across my National Service paybook, blood group card, passes from the Experimental Mobile Column, and *Weights* and *Woodbine* cigarette packets with pencilled names and addresses on them, now faded with time but still quite clear.

Where had the time gone? Here in my hand was the empty cigarette packet with Curly's name and address on it; the friend I'd promised to keep in touch with some 40 years ago, but didn't. I hoped it wasn't too late to make good on my promise.

I contacted the police, the Social Security and pension departments. Each said they would contact me once they had conducted their enquiries. Each day that passed felt like an eternity, yet full of hope, but unfortunately they weren't able to help.

I decided to contact the Post Office at Burton Stather, near Scunthorpe in Lincolnshire, where Curly had lived all those years ago. The postmistress was very helpful and mentioned an elderly lady who cycled every Tuesday to the Post Office and had lived in the village all her life. She would be my best hope. A week later the postmistress informed me that the house Curly had lived in was still in existence, with its original name still intact, but sadly Curly had moved on and no one knew of his whereabouts.

By this time I was feeling rather despondent, but felt I couldn't give up. There was a free newspaper for the Burton Stather area, who said they would help by placing an advertisement. Hey presto, two hours after publication came the news I was waiting for; and Mr White called and said "I believe it's my father you're looking for…" This was fantastic news. Curly was still alive and now living in Bexhill. He and I had more than 50 years of catching up to do.

The next Player's *Weights* packet was that of Charlie Cooper. I telephoned Directory Enquiries and explained that I was looking for an old friend of 50 years ago. It wasn't long before the operator was able to confirm that he still lived at his old address in Barnet. (These were the good old days before the Data Protection Act!) Charlie and I reminisced about our time together and the years that had gone by, and how so much water has passed under the bridge.

My next search was for Brian Birch from Maidenhead. As luck would have it, there was only one B. Birch in the area and via Directory Enquiries he proved easy to trace.

Finding these guys had been quite easy, but now I had the bug and decided to carry on with my quest to find the others I had served with all those years ago.

It has been a long eight years since then, but a remarkable degree of success has been achieved. I couldn't have done this without with the help of Malcolm Bidder, who contacted me having seen his own name on teletext, shortly after I had started using this as a means of contacting people. Malcolm has been a great help, and together we have succeeded in contacting a large number of former comrades.

Of the 160 members of the Experimental Mobile Column, we have managed to make contact with 90. Sadly, we have discovered that 30 more have passed on, leaving around 40 that we still hope to find. It has not been easy, often coming to a dead end, but we feel we must go on, with hope in our hearts that we will find and contact the remaining 40 over the next few years.

In the past seven years we have had six reunions, held at Bourne Hall Museum in Ewell, near Epsom, which have brought us back together.

And so we continue with our quest...

In 1954 we all received a Christmas card which carried the message "we blazed the trail" on the front, and inside was a map showing all the bases we had stayed at. On the back of the card, people had signed their names, which was a tremendous help in finding those I had served with, although to date I haven't been able to find a card with my own name on it!

I cannot remember exactly how many magazines such as saga and free newspapers I have advertised in, but it may well have been in the hundreds.

I would like to take this opportunity to thank David Brooks, the deputy creator of Bourne Hall Museum, Ewell, for his help with the reunions and also in making this book possible.

My thanks go also to Wing Commander John Birch, our president and Malcolm Bidder for his research and never giving up. David Chivers for his journal and developing films, Jim Carson for his journal and help, and for driving 420 miles each way to join us at our reunions, and lastly to all those who have helped by sending photographs and information.

A warm thank you to all of you.

Robin G. Reid, April 2008

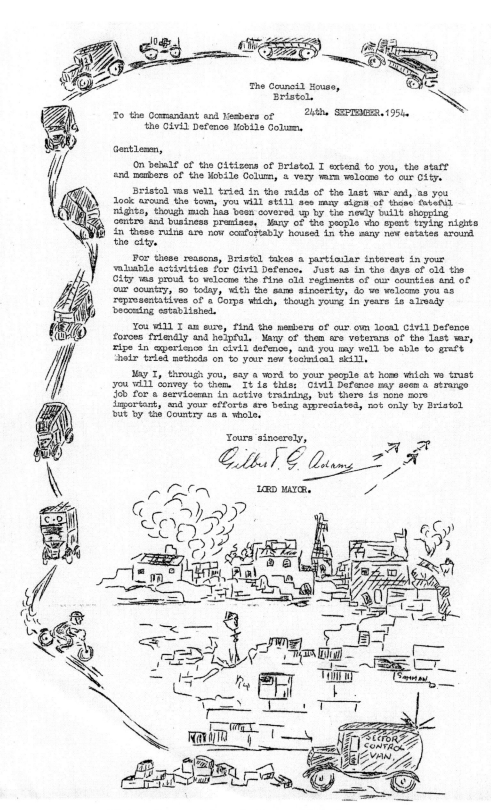

Photo 5. A message from the Mayor of Bristol.

Introduction

You may be surprised to hear that the first official response to nuclear threat in Britain came in 1953 and took place in Epsom with the formation of an Experimental Mobile Column.

In the early 1950s people became aware of the threat posed by the hydrogen bomb. It was realised that if these bombs were dropped on this country, the consequences would be too appalling to be handled by local authorities.

Up to this time, Civil Defence had been handled by local government, and was staffed by volunteers from each neighbourhood. Many councils appointed the Town Clerk or Chief Constable to take charge in the event of an attack.

In 1953 Epsom was the place chosen for the formation of an Experimental Mobile Column. The idea of a column which was mobile and could be rushed to the scene of action deal with serious incidents was not new. There had been services like these in World War II, but now the threat of atomic war made them especially valuable.

The first Experimental Mobile Column was formed at the beginning of 1953 and it was based on the old Kiln Lane site – now occupied by Sainsbury's and a trading estate.

The Column was commanded by Brigadier D.A.L. McKenzie, OBE, DSO. The Brigadier was an ex-Indian army officer, an imposing figure, six feet five inches tall, who succeeded in conveying great enthusiasm to his men. The Column had five officers, a small number of instructors and about 160 National Servicemen. All the serviceman were volunteers in their last year of service, drawn from the RAF and the Army.

The mobile part of the Column consisted of three units, each with one jeep and six vehicles carrying eight men with rescue equipment. There were also two motor cars and four motorcyclists. This was only the beginning; there were plans to establish 100 columns or more to serve near the likely target areas throughout Britain in time of war.

The depot, off East Street, covered several acres, with up-to-date barracks, administrative offices, lecture rooms, and garages. Other rooms were specially designed so that rescue work could be learnt in them.

The Government was keenly interested in the Epsom depot. They knew that the lessons which could be learnt from this first Experimental Column would apply to Civil Defence throughout the country, and to Britain's potential to survive nuclear attack. As Sir David Maxwell Fyfe, the Home Secretary at the time stated, Epsom was the example on which 'would be based the country's defence plans in any future war'.

Though the Column was made up from the RAF and Army, they wore Civil Defence uniforms. Sir David made a public speech to the members of the Column and told them:

'It is no exaggeration to say that your work in the event of war will result n the prevention of much suffering and the maintenance of a high morale out of all proportion to your numbers'. He also asked them to remember the old maxim: 'If you don't need what you have learnt in Civil Defence you have lost nothing, but if you haven't learnt anything in Civil Defence you may lose everything'.

However, the then Mayor of Epsom and Ewell at the time, Alderman C.R.

Bunyan, was most unhappy. He had not been asked to come to the opening of the depot and felt that the Column had acted deliberately by not inviting him and the chairman of the local Civil Defence.

The Home Office replied that it had only been an 'informal ceremony' and the Home Secretary had only gone to address the men. It was arranged that the commandant of the Column would call on the Mayor at the Town Hall when he came to take up his duties.

This situation was finally remedied in 2002 when the Mayor of Epsom and Ewell, Cllr Alan Carlson was invited to attend the first reunion of the Experimental Mobile Column (Epsom) Association.

The Association of former members of the CD Mobile Column has since held regular reunions.

As part of their 2002 re-union they visited the former Epsom site and a plaque was unveiled on the outside wall of the store by Councillor Brian Angus, Mayor of Epsom and Ewell.

Robin G. Reid

1. The Cold War and Civil Defence

by Robin G. Reid

During February 1945 the inhabitants of Bikini Atoll in the Marshall Islands were persuaded to leave their island so that the USA could use it to test nuclear bombs. The Second World War had been brought to a abrupt end by the use of nuclear weapons when atomic bombs were dropped on the Japanese cities of Hiroshima and Nagasaki.

The bombs were relatively small in terms of their destructive power, but both cities suffered massive damage and loss of life.

Tests carried out the following year in Nevada showed the horrifying progress of a nuclear explosion. Time-lapse pictures of a house three-quarters of a mile from the explosion showed first the blinding light, then the shock-wave and the total destruction of the building, all of which took place in under three seconds.

The beginning of the 'Cold War' in the late 1940s prompted the further development of nuclear weapons in the USA, and when the Soviet Union exploded its first bomb in 1949 the nuclear arms race began in earnest.

In November 1952, the first of a new and far more powerful hydrogen bomb, named "Ivy Mike", was tested, causing an explosion more powerful than all the conventional bombs, mines and shells used in both World Wars put together.

The world had entered a new and truly terrifying period of its history.

There was much debate in the UK at the time about whether there was any point in the country trying to defend its people against nuclear attack. Surely, any attempt at Civil Defence in the face of such destructive power would be futile, argued the critics. And besides, the huge amount of money required to do so would be better spent on other things.

The destructive power of such weapons was certainly enormous, replied the supporters of Civil Defence, but beyond the hardest hit areas there would be tens of thousands of citizens who could be saved by the efforts of an effective Civil Defence service.

At Hiroshima over half the people within a mile of the explosion survived, and at Nagasaki almost seven out of ten people within a mile lived – and this was in cities that were entirely unprepared for such an attack.

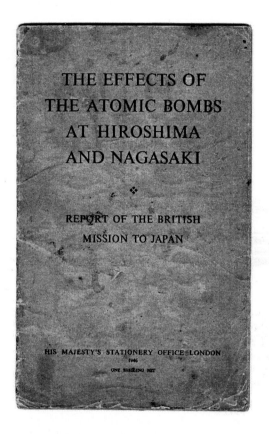

THE EFFECTS OF
THE ATOMIC BOMBS
AT HIROSHIMA
AND NAGASAKI

❖

REPORT OF THE BRITISH
MISSION TO JAPAN

HIS MAJESTY'S STATIONERY OFFICE LONDON
1946
ONE SHILLING NET

Photo 6. This HMSO report prompted some people in the UK to believe it would be worthwhile to invest in Civil Defence measures against a possible nuclear attack.

It was believed casualties among those trapped in wrecked buildings would be greatly reduced if there were trained and equipped rescue parties available to extricate them.

Up to this time, Civil Defence had been handled by local government, staffed by volunteers and run by a local Civil Defence Committee. Most councils appointed the Town Clerk or Chief Constable to take charge in the event of an attack.

Government attempts to recruit volunteers for the civil defence service from among the general public had met with an unenthusiastic response and as a result there were far too few full-time Civil Defence staff to form the mobile rescue columns that the Home Office envisaged.[1]

The Home Office hit upon the solution – to use National Servicemen drawn from the Army and RAF in their second year of service.

During 1951 plans were drawn up for the formation of mobile columns of Civil Defence rescue units, able to be rapidly deployed anywhere in the country where they were needed and fully trained and equipped to rescue people from all manner of disaster situations.

Mobile columns were not a new idea. They had been widely used in World War 2, mostly made up of fire engines, which were sent to render assistance to local forces in areas under heavy attack.

---

[1] Mobile columns of Police and Fire Services had already been formed to reinforce local services in times of need.

Meetings were held between the armed forces and the Home Office. The Army could spare only 50 men but the RAF agreed to supply 100. The Navy were not interested in taking part, asserting that they could not spare any of their own personnel.

The formation of the first Experimental Mobile Column Civil Defence, as it was to be known, was decided at a meeting on 16th April 1952. The working party began in July, with the 1st January 1953 as the target date for formation.

Volunteers were sought from those already serving in the Army and RAF as National Servicemen. They would spend their second year of national service serving in the Column, staying together for a year after completing four months of specialist civil defence training.

This column was to be the first of 100 or more such highly trained columns, covering the whole country.

A Civil Defence site was found at Epsom to enlarge for the Mobile Column Depot and senior fire offices at the Fire College at Dorking began planning the column. Much work was needed on the logistics involved, most of which had been learnt by the fire brigade columns which had operated during the war.

A column had stand on its own, having its own supplies of fuel, food, accommodation, equipment and vehicle repairs. Each of the services was to supply one officer and a few NCOs. The Army would supply the administration and Civil Defence would supply instructors, stores, cooks, etc.

Much discussion was given to the ideal type of men who would make up the column. Men who had been in the building trade or 'labouring types acquainted with building structures" were particularly favoured, and as a result many builders formed the backbone of the rescue services during World War II.

One member of the working party suggested that pioneers should make good rescue men but was told that unfortunately pioneers do not exist in the Army. A pencil note was later added to the minutes: "Yes they do!"

Signalling and radio skills were considered an advantage, along with good character, good physique and intelligence. Above all, the chosen men should have good morale. The choice of men was important as this column was to be the model on which later columns would be built.

The National Servicemen were all to be volunteers and notices were duly placed on noticeboards in RAF and Army camps the length and breath of the country. Men volunteered for many reasons: some to get a posting nearer to their wife, sweetheart or parents; others believed that life at Epsom would be better than that at the camp they were already serving at.

One volunteer from Tonfanau camp in North Wales (who shall remain nameless) was very keen to get away from the snow and frost. The camp had no running water because the reservoir had frozen over and snow had to be melted to wash and shave. There was little to do at the camp and nowhere to go at weekends; there were no buses or trains and worse still, the pubs were all shut. This volunteer 'made his own luck' by altering the names on the camp office posting list of those to be posted to the Mobile Column at Epsom, not believing that he would ever get away with it…

The first column in 1953 was made up of 100 RAF men and 50 men from the Royal Artillery, under the commanded of Brigadier D. A. L. McKenzie, CBE, DSO, He was a 57-year-old, six-foot-five tall ex-Indian Army officer, who succeeded in creating great enthusiasm in his men. The military commander in charge of discipline and administration was Squadron Leader J. A. D. Dodding, RAF GD Branch. The junior officers in charge of the Rescue Units took turns in commanding the column while on tour. The civil defence senior instructor was Major 'Nick' Nicholson (retired), an upright but kindly man, who was well liked by all the men.

The mobile column consisted of three rescue units, each containing one jeep and six rescue vehicles, each carrying eight men with standard rescue equipment, not much different from that used during the war. Each unit also had two staff cars and four motorcyclists. In 1954 a mobile administration section was added.

The Epsom base for the EMC was opened on 4th of January 1953 by Sir Maxwell Fyfe the Home Secretary. During an opening address to the men described the work of the column over the next year as "a most important experiment and on which would be based the country's defence plans in any future war" he added "it is important to the country because our whole future may depend on our readiness to counteract the effects of heavy attacks from the air it is important because unless efficient and effective mobile civil defence services are developed, the task of assisting the static force organised by the local authorities must necessarily devolve upon the armed forces." Sir Maxwell went on: " it is no exaggeration to say that your work in the event of a war will result in the prevention of much suffering and the maintenance of a high morale out of all proportion to your numbers and reminded them of the old slogan if you don't need what you have leant in civil defence you have lost nothing, but if you haven't learnt anything then you may lose everything."

The opening the deport caused great upset at the Town Hall because the Mayor of Epsom and Ewell was not invited. The Town Clerk had been at a Civil Defence conference in London when the Home Secretary spoke of the formation of the column at Epsom and had written to the Home Office asking to be kept informed. The Town Clerk heard nothing more about it until one evening when he heard a report on the wireless saying that the Depot had been officially opened that afternoon.

He wrote to the Home Office rebuking them that:

"No representative of this corporation was invited to be present and I am instructed to lodge a strong protest at this civil discourtesy

And furthermore, the exclusion of the Mayor and Chairman of the Local Civil Defence Committee would appear to be deliberate in this case." The Home Office replied that it had been an informal opening and that the Commanding Officer would visit the Mayor at the Town Hall as soon as his duties would let him.

The men arriving at Epsom were divided into the three rescue units, named 'A' Unit, 'B' Unit and 'C' Unit, plus a Communications Unit and a Motorcyclists Unit.

Each Rescue Unit of about 60 men was divided into teams of six men with their own load/personnel-carrying vehicle. Each Unit had its own Civil Defence instructor and three assistant instructors.

The training ground at Epsom was at the bottom of Kiln Lane, off East Street. At that time, on the left side of Kiln Lane was a football pitch and on the right was the local council rubbish tip, in the quarries left after the removal of clay to make bricks. At the rear of the site was the Epsom–Waterloo railway line.

The Depot consisted of a Civil Defence training centre in a building that was part of the old brickworks and a new, purpose-built training ground of damaged buildings, made to look like a devastated area after a nuclear attack.

The training at Kiln Lane was a mixture of formal lectures, practical training on the purpose-built 'bombsite' and roaring around Epsom Downs in Army vehicles whenever we could get away with it!

The purpose-built bombsite was added to the original Civil Defence centre specifically to train the Mobile Columns. It was built across the old Brickworks site and to the right of it its abandoned buildings and rubbish-filled wasteland, including ponds, gave many extra opportunities to practise various kinds of rescues. The dump and wasteland looked convincingly as if it had been attacked by nuclear weapons. The ruined town was complete, even having half a pub, nicknamed *The Spread Eagle* after the well-known pub of the same name in Epsom at which members of the Column would drink when not on duty.

The training ground is now the site of a trading estate and a Sainsbury's supermarket.

Some of the lectures were by nuclear scientists who were working on the building of Britain's nuclear weapons and others who were monitoring the effects of the bombs dropped on Japan. The information was secret at the time and we were not allowed to take notes.

The physical training in rescue techniques was made as realistic as possible. Some, like Ted Osborn, found it daunting tunnelling through a "collapsed building". They were purpose-built and would not have collapsed any further, but it didn't seem like it at the time! A small army of volunteer 'casualties' were also trained, not only to be able to answer questions such as "where does it hurt?" but also to be able to give realistic displays of panic, aggression, hysteria and other conditions likely to be encountered in real disaster situations. They also had to remain cool while being lowered 100 feet or more out of a ruined building, using only a ladder and rope.

A further area of expertise lay in the preparation of simulated wounds, which added too the realism of the supposed casualties.

A number of men were chosen as drivers and because they needed to be trained to a higher standard than other forces drivers they were sent to the London Transport training centre at Chiswick. While on lunch breaks at Chiswick the trainees would creep away to the skid pan, go upstairs on a double-decker bus and literally 'take it for a spin'. They found this great fun, but more often than not they were caught and told off. While leaning to drive on roads, they used ATV Austins, six of which were lent by the AFS and returned later.

The Column was also issued with two mobile kitchens, which required much labour and were cumbersome, as they burnt coal, so six Army Type 1 petrol burners were borrowed, being much cleaner and easily carried in the kitchen vehicles.

Drivers had to learn to drive in convoys, as vehicles would be travelling in groups at not less 25mph, with a gap of just 30 yards between vehicles – the distance required by the Surrey and Kent police, although other police forces required 80 yards. Training movements in peacetime had to take account of everyday life and other traffic, although there was far less traffic on the roads at that time than there is today. Of course, in time of war or other emergency there would have been special emergency measures initiated and the movement of large columns of vehicles to areas under attack would have taken a different level of priority.

In the event of a real emergency the choice of route would also be most critical and difficult, due to refugees fleeing the area and bomb damage to the area surrounding the main target location.

The weapons of this new era of warfare would also present new problems of radioactive or chemical fallout which would further restrict access.

The movements of the Column did, however, produce a few lighter moments…

The 1953 column of 76 vehicles, 14 motorcycles and two cable trailers must have been quite a sight. One small boy, upon seeing the cable trailers being towed by, called out: "Oh mummy, look at the window cleaners!"

On parking in the market place in Stockton-on-Tees, some little boys clambered on the running board of the Commandant's Humber staff car. Sticking his head through the window, one boy asked, "Are you the boss?"

"Yes," the commandant replied.

"Well then mister, can we see the tigers?"

It was not only the onlookers who had their amusing moments, as Malcolm Bidder recalls of a stopover at Washington, County Durham…

The exercise for that day had been cancelled, so a group of the lads decided to have a game of cards in one of the meeting rooms before wandering off into town. After about twenty minutes the voice of the senior NCO, Sergeant Harry Stubley, could be heard shouting: "Outside on parade – a maintenance day!"

"We opened the end windows, jumped out and legged it," Malcolm recalls.

"The following day Harry stopped me and asked me if I had been in the meeting room the previous morning, giving me the chance to wriggle."

"Why? What was going on in the meeting room sergeant?" I replied innocently.

"There were five poker hands on the table," he replied, "the windows were wide open and the curtains were gently swinging in the breeze. I thought it was the Marie Celeste!"

The Column had its own motorcycle escorts, who underwent their training at the Military Police training school at Woking. Police escorts were sometimes provided from the outskirts of larger cities and towns to the site of the exercises, but even so, on one memorable occasion one Rescue Unit meet another going in the opposite direction.

During its two years in existence the Column completed 16 tours, during which it visited every one of the civil defence districts in England, Scotland and Wales. Exercises were held in every area, along with inspections, parades and 'publicity days'.

In 1954 *Picture Post* magazine went along to watch the column in action at Swansea and wrote that they "had no doubt as to its value and that the local civil defence we in full agreement."

The system seemed now to have been approved and in July the Home Secretary announced that a part-time Commander-in-Chief Mobile Columns was to be appointed. It was intended that if war came that perhaps 100-200 columns would be established near to likely target areas.

The bomb that fell on Hiroshima killed 78 thousand people and destroyed everything within a half mile radius but the hydrogen bombs of 1954 were 750 times more powerful. Some people felt that against such weapons there could be no defence and that the money required to pay for such defence could be better spent. The only viable defence, they argued, was to agree never to use these weapons.

It was during a visit to Coventry that the Column ran into political controversy. The City Council at Coventry had been debating whether Civil Defence was a waste of time and money and stood in the way of nuclear disarmament. In fact, the Council had voted to close down its Civil Defence Committee. The man who moved the resolution in Coventry was Alderman Sidney Stringer, Leader of the Council's Labour Group. They believed that the only solution was a meeting of the great powers and the renunciation of the terrible weapons, or at lest the guarantee on our part not to use them first. Others asked: "Would that be enough?"

Stringer thought it would.

"You have to trust people," was his answer.

Several Labour members of the council were planning to visit Stalingrad, to see if people of that city shared their beliefs.

However, Coventry did not lose its Civil Defence, it was take over by three Commissioners appointed by the Home Office and the local 'rates' were increased to pay for them. Other councils followed, including Cloune District Council in Derbyshire and Tottenham in London. Other councils took the middle ground and declared that if Civil Defence could be proved worthwhile then it should be taken up by National rather than local government.

In a 1953 white paper Civil Defence was stressed as being an essential part of our defence planning and in late 1954 a Government memo stated: "there is no distinction today between civil defence and home defence. Men and women, if they want to do their duty, will join what is called civil defence. They will be led by their civil experts and officials. By their side, trained in the ordinary knowledge of rescue work, demolition, fire-fighting and the rest, will be all the armed forces of the Crown. These forces would be under the Commander-in-Chief Home Forces and to link with the static civilians and service formations will be the formations of the new mobile columns of the Royal Mobile Defence Force.

But by the end of 1954 the Government had changed its mind. The Mobile Columns were to be disbanded and instead it was decided to train 7,000 to 8,000 RAF reservists, who would undergo a fortnight's annual training at Epsom and at a further base in

Lancashire. The same number again would be trained the following year. The numbers would double and eventually 100,000 men would be available for Civil Defence in the event of an emergency.

This action was taken because the Government felt it was better to have a potential force of a 100,000 men available than a full-time force far fewer in number. The new Commander-in-Chief Mobile Columns was left with no mobile columns to command. The *Picture Post* wrote:

"All the good work that the Mobile Column is doing in raising the standards of local forces, publicising Civil Defence, in giving men knowledge or movement, and in research, will come to an end. Instead there will be substituted a remote system which will take years to come to any use."

It added:

"The column cost only £100,000 in 1953 and will probably cost a lot less this year.

There is surely room for the column to operate along side the new system."

This view was shared by some councils. The Town Clerk of the City of Exeter wrote to the Under Secretary of State at the Home Office:

"At the recent exercise held in this City in which the mobile Column took part, the regional officer informed the controller designate that it was proposed to discontinue the Mobile Column in its present form in the near future. The matter was discussed at the last meeting of the Civil Defence Committee, when I was instructed to inform you that they view the decision with considerable concern, having regard to the immense value the Column has proved to the Civil Defence organisation in connection with training, and to request that further consideration be given to the matter."

In 1954 the Column did cost less – just £60,000 – but sadly this year was to be the Column's last.

2. My Experiences with the EMC 1953-54

by Malcolm Bidder

I reported to RAF Cardington on 6th August 1953 to commence my two years National Service. Large hangars there had housed airships, including the R101, before the war. After six days kitting out, etc, we were posted to RAF Hednesford for basic training. Eight weeks later and very much fitter, we assembled to receive our postings.

One of the lads thought he was going to Germany until it was explained to him that Weston Zoyland was actually in Somerset!

Six of us were posted to 216 Maintenance Unit, Sutton Coldfield and five of us disliked it! You could say that 216 Unit kept the RAF on the move. It supplied bicycles and bicycle parts to all the other RAF stations. There were huge sheds with hundreds of upright bicycles, hanging and greased, ready for action, along with thousands of spare parts such as chains and sprockets, all with reference numbers starting with 61-bY.

After a few weeks I observed a queue at the noticeboard. The notice read:

"Volunteers are required for the ARMY/RAF Civil Defence Experimental Mobile Column – 100 from the RAF and 50 from the ARMY."

The odds seemed rather long, but, as they say – "if you're not in it, you can't win it…"

Several weeks later we were informed that two of us had been selected: a lad from Newcastle, Donald Millar, and myself. The general opinion was that we had been chosen because we were expendable!

I duly arrived at the Civil Defence depot at Kiln Lane, Epsom. Walking around the camp, I found what at first appeared to be a bomb-site. Further inspection showed it to be a purpose-built bomb-site – in half of a hotel called *The Spreadeagle*.

The Civil Defence instructors were the top available men. We had classroom lessons and then practical work, Monday to Friday (as a bonus we had every weekend off) for three months. Exercises, followed until we were ready to tour.

The Column consisted of three units, each with six rescue vehicles, Land Rovers, motorcyclists, signals, transport, catering and general service.

Eight tours were undertaken, including Aberdeen in the north, Plymouth in the south-west, Canterbury and Norwich in the east, Swansea in the west and many towns and cities in between. We had our own civilian catering staff, with a top-class chef.

To cover smaller exercises the column would be split. On these occasions catering would be undertaken by the local WRVS – and what a splendid job they did often in difficult conditions.

We were very well received by most local authorities. Drinks, Cinema tickets and other goodies were supplied.

Coventry was the exception. The local council had dismissed civil defence as a waste of time and money. The *Picture Post* of 16th October 1954 devoted a two-page

spread to the argument, although the reporter was obviously on our side – he wrote that anyone who witnessed the Swansea exercise could not fail to be impressed by the expertise of the Mobile Column.

Many local authorities wrote in support of retaining the Mobile Column, but the Home Office decision was to disband it on 31st December 1954.

Several years ago, I replied to an advertisement placed by Robin G. Reid (the Association secretary) who had been in touch with the Epsom Museum to arrange a reunion of the Column. I accepted the post of researcher and over the coming years I followed up all the leads that were available to track down former personnel of the Mobile Column. Autographs on a 1954 Christmas menu, general records of births at the Devon Family History Centre in Exeter, *Saga* magazine and the *RAF News,* followed by the electoral roll on computer disc. This enabled us to locate 90 members. A further 34 are no longer with us, a further 40 remain a mystery still…

Photo 7. Double-page-spread in the _Picture Post_ of 16/10/54.

3.   A Mobile Column Diary 1953-4

by David J. Chivers

This diary was written close on 50 years ago and many terms used were abbreviations we used at the time , for instance a QL was a type of BEDFORD lorry, 202 was the number of my van, CRV was a Column Rescue Vehicle and a PCV was a Person Carrying Vehicle, and so on. The main point of my keeping this "log Book" was to record my life on the Column and on reflection I think it is a fair reminder of how things were. I was at Epsom for the whole of 1953 but only some of 1954, so my recollections feature only part of 1954, but Jim Carson's memoir (which follows) also covers the latter part of 1954. I hope you enjoy my memories of life on the Experimental Mobile Column.

March 17th 1953

On January 1st I came to Epsom to serve with the Civil Defence on the Experimental Mobile Column, which is to tour England this year.

We were given a navy-blue uniform bearing our crest on the breast pocket. The Home Secretary came down and launched us on our way. Then things really started to happen. The three rescue groups went off to C.D. schools on courses but we in Communications and Recce stayed here and took a course with Major Nicholson on fire-fighting, first-aid, atomic warfare and rescue work. That basic finished we started our three-week driving course with London Transport. Our three weeks were very full, with plenty of reversing and driving in the heart of London. We took skid control at Chiswick and learnt how the engine works so as to give us some idea of how to carry out minor repairs. Then on January 30th we took the test, which I managed to pass.

Next came the signals course. We wee now a small group under the leadership of Corporal Watkinson, learning how to lay telephone lines and how to operate walkie-talkies and wireless sets. Now came our first trip out, we journeyed to Croydon, where we worked with walkie-talkies on the sewerage farm in thick mud and in the dark. As we improved we went out on little trips for practice in wireless procedure and map reading.

March has found us enjoying very nice sunny weather as we journey around this area in small convoys with DRs guiding us.

Today we had our first real exercise. Comms and Recce went out together with a mobile kitchen a food distribution van and one of the little office vans. The headquarters was set up a Sunningdale, where we put up the aerial and established a wireless base and set the kitchen to work on our dinner. Then the groups set out – A, B and C to Woking, Staines and Windsor. My van [GHX 202] with my co-driver David Walter and F/O Gardner set off for Windsor; with us came Jack Boyd and Corporal Hadaway as a RECCE party. We found our base and parked in a field near a farm. We could not get very good contact with the base though, due to 'skreening'. At 13.45the dinner arrived, which we ate standing around the vans. The menu: warm pea soup, steak pie, peas and mash, followed by peaches and custard with plenty of coffee. This feast finished we toured around Windsor trying to locate the base. This failed, so we set off on the homeward road. We were met by two Landrovers who escorted us back to Epsom.

April 23rd 1953

A great step up in progress has been taken since I last wrote. The rescue range is now finished and the rescue groups have been spending most of their time out there perfecting their rescue tactics. Last week they all had a night exercise. At about 8 o'clock bombs were heard exploding and a red glow appeared in the sky above the range; fires were burning in the houses and the toy factory was a real blaze. Wounded people could be heard among the ruins moaning and crying.

Then, around the corner, came a rescue group, which soon was parked, with red lights on each corner and floodlights. This was followed by a few brief orders and the parties were away with lamps, ladders, etc to work in the dark. I heard said later that they enjoyed working at night more than during the day.

Today at 8am this base was full of life. Engines were all ticking over and the groups were all lined up ready for the first big Column move. At the lead was the Deputy Commandant's car, followed by the two Army rescue groups. At a 10 minute gap behind them came the RAF rescue group and behind that came the Admin echelon with the QL bringing up the rear.

On leaving the base we were escorted through Epsom by the Metropolitan Police. Our route took us along the Leatherhead bypass [the A246] to Merrow and on along the Guildford bypass to the A321 and then to Pirbright, a distance of about 27 miles. On arrival at Pirbright we pulled into a camping ground, which had already been laid out by an advance party, and parked in the places marked for us. After a break we pitched our tents for the Commandant to see. He seemed quite pleased with our efforts, so we put a jerk into it and were packed up again by lunchtime.

The mobile kitchen was improved very much during the past week and we were given a very nice lunch. The menu today was a mug of oxtail soup, cold meat, tomatoes, beetroot, pickles and mashed potatoes. Jelly and chocolate blancmange and tea.

At 2pm we were all set to drive back. I worked the set while F/O Gardiner drove.

Tomorrow we are having the dress rehearsal for Monday's demonstration when the Home Secretary is coming to see us at work before we go on tour next Friday May 1st.

The whole set up is very much better everyone knows what to do without any bother. The weather is very nice and everything is very nice apart from the one thing and that is a smell which is given us by the Epsom And Ewell Corporation. I suppose they want to be helpful and get us used to working near broken sewers.

April 27th 1953

This morning everyone was very busy cleaning up the camp area and washing their trucks. David and I gave ours the once over both inside and out to mark the special occasion.

At 2.45pm everyone was on the spot. Rescue groups were all lined up and ready for action. Recce were already on the range waiting for the big bang. From where I was situated I saw all the guests arrive. By a few minutes to three the garage was nearly full of private cars. At 3pm the Mayor and Mayoress of Epsom arrived and just after them came Lord Lloyd. He came as deputy of the Home Secretary, who was detained in the House of Commons.

The Commandant gave his opening address, then the big bang went up and as I stood outside my wireless van, the boys of 'C' flashed past me laden with stretchers, hatchets, saws and crowbars as they ran across the debris to the place where they were to carry out a rescue according to the group leader's instructions.

After a while our guests moved onto the range to take a closer look at what was going on. Newspapermen were there taking photographs and the BBC were making recordings.

The big laugh came when our first-aid instructor from the Surrey County Council was found in an Anderson shelter dressed up as an old lady. As they brought 'her' out, she was waving her handbag, calling for 'her Fred' and complaining because she 'had only cleaned her windows yesterday'.

When all was finished Lord Lloyd addressed us. He said he was very impressed by what he had seen. In closing, he wished us every success with our tour and hoped we would enjoy ourselves as we journeyed up and down the country.

TOUR ONE ~ 1st May 1953

At 9.30am this morning the Mobile Column moved out from Epsom depot on its first tour. It was pouring with rain as we moved into East St, where on the corner stood two of the typists and the telephonist to wave us on our way.

We drove to Reigate, where the mayor and his corporation took the salute at the march-past. From there we moved on to Oxted, where there was another march-past (in our trucks), still in pouring rain. The poor Recce chaps were wet through. At about 1.45 pm we arrived at Wouldham Camp, where we are to stay until Wednesday.

2.5.53

This afternoon the column went on a publicity tour of Rochester and Chatham. At Chatham, 'C' Group paraded in front of the town hall and were inspected by the Mayor. After his address we were given tea, which was thoroughly enjoyed by all. Then at 5pm we drove back to Wouldham Camp in the evening sunshine. The view was much more interesting than when we arrived yesterday.

3.5.53

Today being Sunday we took things easy. We gave the vans a shine up ready for this afternoon. At 11 o'clock we had a light lunch, consisting of salad. Then when the Humber ran around camp sounding its horn everyone ran to where the group was parked. At about 12.30 we moved out under police escort for Rochester Airport, which was to be our rendezvous. We were not there long before we moved into Chatham, where 'C' Group went to the Marine Barracks to rescue some 50 casualties. The other groups went to other parts of the town, one crossing the river Medway in boats.

'C' Group finished first, so we set off back to camp, soon to be followed by the other groups. Our first real exercise seems to have been quite successful.

5.5.53

Today the police had to go with us on their own at taking the column through the Medway towns and back. During the exercise everything went very well, apart from Lieutenant Patton's leading vehicle, the occupants of which were watching a police 'lady' instead of her signals. As a result there was a little upset for a moment. Order was soon restored and the Column arrived back at Wouldham in one long piece. During the afternoon we took it *very* easy on the grass, enjoying the warm sun.

Yesterday cannot pass unmentioned… We were rushed into Chatham where a so-called 'heavy air raid' had just taken place. 'C' Group was sent to the Naval base, where we had some 50 'casualties' to attend to. Groups B, and A were called in to give us extra help. After lunch we were inspected by two high ranking officers from the Navy and the Marines.

6.5.53

Today the E.M.C. moved to Brighton. On route we marched passed the mayor of Maidstone and at Tunbridge Wells we were inspected by the Mayor, who afterwards joined the staff for lunch, which was prepared in the Mobile Kitchens. During an address the Mayor presented us with the Civil Defence flag. A special note on the flag: it was the first C.D. flag ever made and is also the *largest* one there is. After lunch we moved on towards our aim, which we reached in good time. The police led us through Brighton and on to the seafront, where we were inspected by their Lady Mayoress (a very kind person) who then took us to the Royal Pavilion, where she entertained us to a super tea. Speeches followed. Thanks to the Mayoress, as she was the first Mayor to address us instead of the people above our heads.

The Commandant replied and thanked the Mayoress for the very warm welcome which she and the people of Brighton had given us. There were unfortunately one or two people, mainly local tradesmen, who were on their afternoon deliveries and met the Column on more than one occasion. I'll not mention their words of greeting!

At Warren Farm School, where we are staying, we found the local CD HQ. They have a very nice club in part of the school, at which they held a dance in our honour.

7.5.53

Today is our rest day. The C.O. has visited us and given us our pay and the Council have given us two very nice guide books, so we are all set for a day in town. Tomorrow we return to Epsom in time for lunch.

8.5.53

We returned to Epsom via Crawley, where we had a march past. All were in Camp by 13.00 hrs after a few break-downs on route.

TOUR 2 ~ 17th May 1953

At 9am last Thursday we left Epsom on Tour Two. We had quite a long run via Guildford, Farnham and Winchester. The long route was taken due to other forces also on the move. Orders were issued to the effect that if we were attacked the Column was to split up and turn off the road, so as to minimise the extent of damage.

Late afternoon the Column arrived at Titchfield RAF Station, where it set up its base.

On Friday everyone stood easy, but on Saturday mid-day Southampton was bombed. The damage was in 3 areas. 'C' Group advance party was sent to the Nurses Hostel, where a 3-storey wing had been badly damaged.

On arrival at the site, F/O Gardner and I, plus two other Recce parties, entered the building. The stairs were found to be still intact so we did the obvious thing and used them. Mr Gardner and I took the top floor. where we found some casualties with severe injuries. I was then given orders to call for extra help from HQ. The reply soon came that two rescue parties were on their way to join us.

Recce now completed, I abandoned my walkie-talkie and did what I could to help with rescue. I took out a walking casualty with a burnt arm. Then I found a young lady under a bath with a crushed arm. I got her out and gave her bicarbonate of soda to drink and put her arm in a sling. Sergeant Worth took her name, etc, and took her out.

Upstairs I found a pile of water tanks so I climbed over them and looked around and in one room I saw a lady with a piece of burnt wood across her legs. I moved it and found she was in a very dangerous state. One leg was badly cut and the other was hanging off from below the knee. The case was given priority and Corporal Bowden's party soon had her out to the doctor, who had a first aid post near at hand and was able to give morphea and do the necessary.

Exercise *Minerva* ended at 4 o'clock with 16 casualties all out in good time. Food and drink were next on the list so we moved to where the WVS of the Southampton area had their "Food Flying Squad" waiting to serve us with tea, sandwiches and cakes.

At 7pm the Column – with the Fire Service at its head and the Food Flying Squad at its tail – marched past the Mayor and Civic Centre in Southampton before returning to base.

Sunday

Open to the public and CD of Hampshire today. The weather is very unsettled so the inspection by two Army Officers was called off and they just had a little natter with us. Then we sat in our vans for the rest of the morning, answering questions and having long chats with the "old boys" who show a great interest in this whole setup.

One old fellow was very upset because he said we should not mix our service drill and our CD drill together when the public are watching for fear we might create a wrong impression on the public and this turn any might be recruits away.

21.5.53

On Monday evening we moved out from Titchfield and set off for Portsmouth. Exercise *Discovery* was underway. It was pouring with rain when we arrived at the sub control. 'C' Group received instructions to proceed to Hawke Road, where we found quite a spread out area of damage, including three air-raid shelters. Unfortunately, nearly all the casualties were dead. Tea was provided by the WVS. We reached our base at about 11.15 pm, had some soup and fell into bed.

Tuesday we were up at 6am. During the morning we washed and cleaned the vans ready for a publicity drive through Portsmouth and Portchester. After tea the Rescue sections received a call for help at Exercise *Discovery* (part 2). This time 'C' Group were sent to Victoria Naval Barracks. I took the walkie-talkie and went with the chief into the red brick 'shell' and up the stone staircase. The floors were a bit dodgy in places, as there was not much support underneath. However, the report was made and sent to HQ by David Walter, who was working the set. The extra parties were soon on the spot and work was going at a fare rate. The Food Flying Squad brought us tea and sandwiches.

Our task was completed with 15 mins in hand, so again we had a happy and proud officer. Back at RV the Food Flying Squad served us with a hot meal. The WVS certainly know how to cook! The BBC visited us and made some recordings. We returned to base at about 10.30 pm again rather tired.

4.6.53

Today, as quite a change, five of the Column's vans went to Woolwich for a carnival. It took three hours to cover eight miles. Thousands of people were cheering all along the route, so we felt that we knew how the Queen felt on Tuesday. Quite a nice trip back via Loughborough Junction – twice! (After a wrong turn.) Arrived Epsom at midnight.

Tour 3 – June 9th 1953

On Sunday we moved from Epsom to RAF Benson, where we were camping under canvas. On Monday we moved on to Birmingham, where the VCH's were parked on the fairground while the boys slept at Aston Villa Football ground. I was on guard at the fairground where we heated water with a blowlamp for a wash. We made a bed up in our vans and slept quite well when not on stag.

Tuesday we were on again northwards towards Manchester and parked at an RA camp at High Leah.

On Wednesday I.C.I. was 'bombed', so 'B' Group with the QL moved to Northwich. When we arrived we were surrounded by chimneys, overhead pipes, power station engines, railway trucks, and in other words a typical factory that deals with chemicals and dust and muck. I went with Mr Brown and as we made our way across to the centre of the damage we met a man who was delirious. He told us he had been working on the site for 4 days so we sat him down and put a man to look after him. A Tech Manager came up and told us roughly what had happened. He told us who was in charge but we found the man had been trapped in the building and they were all asking for him. The Rescue Parties were called up and set to work. With the aid of a hacksaw I helped cut away into a boiler house where we found a number of dead.

A number of the casualties were violent and kept trying to get up and go home and made real menaces of themselves. Then a crowd of screaming women arrived trying to find their husbands so more Rescue persons had to be called in to control them. There was a gas attack which lasted half and hour. During that time we found out that working with gas masks was quite hard going.

At 9.30 we had cleared it all up and had a good sing going back in the Q.L.

Exercise 'Alpha' – 14.6.53

As the advance party pulled into the square at Rochdale this morning, everywhere was very quiet; a typical Sunday morning. The church bells were ringing at the parish church and the Salvation Army band could be heard playing its way about the streets.

The chiefs were at a conference in the town hall when bombs were heard exploding. Under a police guide, 'C' Group moved to Clover Hill (a cotton mill burned out about a year ago). Policemen were bringing out casualties when we arrived and the DCO was a big

policeman who had his HQ in a police radio car. The building, of steel frame construction, was a 'shell'. More parties were sent for as the work was estimated to require more help than was at present available.

A lady doctor, nurses and ladies in St John's uniform worked on casualties while the rescue sections climbed floor after floor up through the building. Ambulances came and went and still the wounded kept pouring out.

The WVS provided us with tea and biscuits between our jobs. Then when the last casualty was brought out and the doctor had certified the bodies in the mortuary as dead the exercise ended. The police guide took us back to the camp and we had our lunch.

During the afternoon the local CD people came up and looked over the Column. One was so keen as to take out a walkie-talkie and listen to a message from the L67 and then vice-versa.

Exercise Bang – 16.6.53

This exercise took place in Oldham, in a dirty, dusty building that was without windows. Searchlights and torches were used. Casualties were found in tunnels and in most awkward places. It was gone

11pm when we returned to base, so we soon retired to bed, not in the tent but on the van lockers.

The camp is now a bog; the rain which has kept us company nearly all the time we have been at Rochdale has just about washed everything away, but there are still a few laughs had, despite everything.

I should have mentioned that this afternoon we went on one of our mobile marchpasts-cum-inspections in Manchester. The whole column lined up in front of the tall black town hall, which was still decorated with red white and blue bunting from the Coronation. Just after the clock had struck two the Mayor and company came out and inspected us. Tomorrow we move out.

17.6.53

This morning we bade farewell to Rochdale and move the Lytham via Bolton and Preston, where we are camping at 5PDC RAF. It is a real RAF station which made the Army chaps open their eyes. The mess is super with wonderful food; curtains at the windows, flowers on the table and all the little things that make a dining room pleasant. The billets are very nice too. During the evening I visited Blackpool, which I liked, but would not fancy spending a holiday there.

20.6.53

Before leaving Blackpool we had a demonstration for the public at the Hotel Metropole, where two groups from each section took part. Down on the prom, the Mayor of Blackpool inspected a column of vehicles, one of each kind. On Friday morning we stopped in Southport, where the Mayor gave the officers a little party in his parlour. David and I quite enjoyed the commentary that Mr Gardner gave us, in a northern accent, on his return. We had a very good packed lunch and arrived at Liverpool Regimental Barracks about 4 pm.

Yesterday I was one base set while the column went out via the Mersey Tunnel on a drive and an exercise. During the evening the Home Secretary visited us and said that he was pleased with how things were going.

Exercise 'Columbine' – 21.6.53

Today for seven hours one of the largest CD exercises ever took place in Liverpool. There were three incidents: one at Gladstone Docks where a ship, the *Empress of Canada*, had been hit, another at Dingle oil works and the third at Lister Power Station. The latter was the one to which 'C' Group was sent. We had made our first reports and work was under way when a bomb or something hit our van, causing us to be 'killed' and the radio to go out of action, so before we had time to sit back and take it easy we were whipped away on rescue work! They engaged us on hauling on ropes, which raised stretchers up through the building where they were received by other members of the party and carted away.

After lunch we went on a second exercise on one of the training grounds, where, for the first time on these tours, we met with fire. We returned to base at about 6.30pm and soon retired to bed. During the afternoon I was kept very busy on set as I seemed the only van on column who could make contact all round with everyone else, thus I found myself doing a great deal of relay work to and from other stations to M2CDA or in other words the Q.L. at H.Q.

23.6.53

On Monday we went on a very nice joyride to Warrington. It was a duty trip, but it was a very nice evening and not much traffic about made it enjoyable. On arrival at Warrington we drove into the park and lined up, open to the public. Children enjoyed working a short telephone that we fitted up for them. We were given sandwiches and tea before we returned.

Today is our rest day. John and David C and I went to Liverpool and on to New Brighton for the afternoon. We had a nice time, the best bit being when we went flying in rockets. The first time up I could not get down but on the second flight I flew up and down, quite enjoying myself as a U/T pilot. Next we had a try at being air gunners and to finish up we went on a Super Figure 8. During the evening we walked around, looking at the lights and sights! Tomorrow we set off back to Epsom.

26.6.53 - We left Liverpool at 7.15am and passed through the Mersey Tunnel before the traffic became too thick. Little lamps set in the wall lit the way along the 4-way tunnel. We passed crossroads and traffic lights all down under the River Mersey. All I could find wrong was the blue mist of exhaust smoke. On down the country en route for Epsom moved the Column, halting for a night at Kidderminster and Oxford. On the last day's run we visited Sandhurst, where people looked at our kit while we had lunch under the trees beside the lake.

Then, during the last few miles of the 800-odd miles covered, one of the D/Rs had a pile-up and ruined his bike, but he was only slightly hurt. Now for a long weekend at home!

Tour 4 – 12.7.53

On the 6th we left Epsom on Tour 4. We had a wet start but it soon cleared up and by the time we reached Watford it was quite fine. Our journey took us past the DeHaviland area works at Hatfield and on up country to Cambridge, where we stayed the night under canvas, in a park slap in the middle of town. One outstanding feature was that everyone seemed to ride bicycles. On the 7th we moved on another 100-odd miles. On route we stopped at Grantham, where the Mayor gave an address before inspecting the Column, which he said "sparkled with efficiency". Quite how, I don't know! We stayed the night at Ruffold Abbey, miles from anywhere. We travelled through the smallest and largest counties in England during this trip.

On the morning of the 8th we moved to Sherborne-in-Elmet, a little village about 15 miles from Leeds. We are in houses which have been converted into small rooms to take one person. It has been

quite nice to be alone for a few days and to do just what you like.

Yesterday and today have been a dead loss so far as I am concerned. There have been two big exercises in Leeds, but I have not seen any of it as no communications have been used. Since this tour began we have been in the Admin Echelon and not with the Groups, which I feel is silly, as that's where we have always been so far and now I know just what is required of us there. However, the Chiefs seem to be trying out something else.

I was out yesterday, as a relay station between here and Leeds, during the afternoon, but there was no traffic being passed, so I returned to base.

This afternoon we are going to reel in the wires from the temporary exchange we fitted up and take down the big aerial so that we too can have a rest day tomorrow before moving on to Hull on Tuesday.

Exercise 'Hannibal' July 21st 1953

Today is a rest day. We are situated just outside Guisbrough, surrounded on three sides by the Cleveland hills, which are a range of hills on the Yorkshire moors. The view is quite a change, but at the same time one could be in Axbridge, looking at the Mendips. I have found

Yorkshire to be more beautiful than I expected.

Yesterday we went on one of our "drives" to Stockton-on-Tees and West Hartlepool where the respective Mayors inspected the Columns and talked to us (quite a change).

Sunday was said to have been one of our big do's, but after loading ourselves with tools, spare batteries, etc, we did not seem to do anything. As we arrived at an incident, it either was closed, not working or closed just after we arrived. All that seemed to happen was plenty of deployment and interchanging of groups. Exercise 'Hannibal' took place in Middlesbrough.

Our stay in Hull was based at the Evans Fraser HQ, about two miles outside the city. There were two exercises in Hull, but ATVs were not used. (I should have mentioned we did go with our GP CDRs. In Excercise 'Hannibal' on the old method of one ATV and one CRV from each group going first to the incident and more were then called for from the incident). At Hull the Comms Section was kept busy receiving and sending messages to the Hull Controller and to the Regional Controller in Leeds. The QL and CDL was based on the lawn and was in contact with the two staff cars.

One 'hot spot' came when the "Col Cdr" was taken ill and someone else had to step in and take his place. Since then, the Col Cdr has kept someone else informed about what is going on, so there would be a smooth takeover.

During an inspection a small boy was heard to ask the Brigadier if he was the "Boss". He replied that he was. "Well then," was the reply. "What is this? A circus?" Someone tactfully told the boy that if he walked to the back he would see a tiger!

Exercise 'Trent' – 27.7.53

Going for petrol on July 21st we passed the 3,000 mile mark so far covered since I took over the van. Since we came on Tour in May we have covered 2,064 miles.

We are now at Rufford Abbey again; we came here on the 22nd. It was our longest trip so far, we covered 120 miles. On Friday we went to Nottingham for an exercise. One group to one of three incidents. Mr Gardner is now Column Commander for a few days, so Sergeant Worth was i/c 'C' Group. Our incident was in Edwards Lane at quite a big house. The Fire Service were there, City Ambulances, Police and Local CD forces. The WVS laid on the usual good cup of tea. Our work was quite the same as usual a Tele 'L' had to be laid out to the DCO's post and then we just sent the reports through and received our instruction from Column H.Q.

We had dinner at the Police and Fire H.Q. in the centre of the city. Dave and I received an invitation from the City Fire Chief to come and look over the station and see the control room. So, today being a rest day, we went. I was taking Derek out on driving instruction so we made Nottingham our first port of call. We drove into the yard and parked out of any bodies way and then looked around.

We found the gentlemen we were looking for and he took us to the control room where we were shown all the systems and set ups that they have there.

One device which I found very interesting worked on a line that the firemen would be on the spot before the fire started. A thermostat in roofs or on ceilings of rooms in big stores or factories has two metal plates a fraction of an inch apart if a small fire starts in a room the temperature rises, the metal contracts, makes a contact and a fire alarm goes off in the control room saying where it is. On arrival at the place another panel at the door or somewhere on the ground floor shows which room or rooms the fire is in. In short a very good idea. Then into the station, where we were shown the ins and outs of all the fire engines. While in the control room a 999 call came in. The engine was away in 35 seconds!

Last Saturday afternoon we were inspected by the Mayor and Sheriff of Nottingham. In the evening, after tea given us by the Midland Convoy Food Flying Squad, we moved into action on a big exercise on the Clifton Housing Estate. As we made our way through the City and across the river Trent we could see a column of black smoke rising into the sky. When we arrived the Fire Service were working on the fire and our chaps had the task of rescuing all the people from houses covering a very large area. We had the task of laying six telephone lines, but very little radio was used. We drove back in the dark at midnight.

Sunday afternoon we went on a publicity drive to Mansfield, where we were inspected by the Mayor. Radio was on and what with female wardens and Corporal Watkinson on the set we had quite a laugh!

Exercise 'Concentrate' – 30.7.53

At 11am on Tuesday the 28th the Column left Rufford Abbey and proceeded via side roads which offered plenty of cover to Derby. We arrived at a point just outside at 1 pm and had a hurried lunch then 'C' group moved to an incident at Mark Eaton Park where we had the taste of clearing casualties. I started to lay a telephone line form the DCO's post to the Warden's Post but due to road crossing it became useless so I set up a walkie-talkie link for them.

Then Mr Gardner sent me to start work in a room where people were trapped by a fallen ceiling. However, by the time I had removed one and freed two other a rescue party had come to take over. I then returned to our van and stayed with David, helping with messages until the close of the incident.

Evening came and we had an evening meal. At about 6.30pm the air raid warning went (a real one) all over the city. It sort of set us on edge, even though we knew it was only an exercise. Mr Patton was Col Commander, so his group came and worked with C Group. 'A' group remained at the R.V.

We arrived at the place to find local men already working. A block of housing had been hit. One side at the back had been blown out and nearly all the windows had been blown out or smashed. All was going fine when a UXB was found. Some of the CRVs had been moved, but two remained. Whistles blew and everyone

had to run for shelter. We waited, then came some explosions – about seven or eight all told. Then one end of the block burst into flames. Smoke and flames poured through the windows and screaming could be heard from within. Then, in the distance, came the sound of clanging bells and the wail of a siren as fire engines made their way to the fire.

No sooner than they had arrived an automatic water tower was going into action and pouring water into the heart of the fire. Hose pipes were everywhere as we made our way back to continue rescue work. Midnight and we were still working.

The floodlights, which David, Mr Booker and I had fixed up, were working very well, four 300-watt bulbs in reflectors give a very nice light.

Just after midnight 'A' group arrived to take over while we returned to the RV for tea and cake. At 1.30 am we went to sleep but were woken up again just after 2.30am to drive back to base – a good 30 miles away. The police quite enjoyed themselves taking us back; we were going to the right round the roundabouts and going at about 30mph, as we were about the only things on the road. We reached base at 5 am on Wednesday 29th.

Exercise 'Flash' – 31.7.53

All day Wednesday we spent sleeping. In the evening we went to Ollerton Pit and had a shower, which I enjoyed very much. We returned and went to bed again!

Thursday "Sergeant" Pearson came up with Major to pay us before we left on our last job this side of August.

We left Rufford Abbey and did a tour of the neighbouring towns and ended up at Ilkstone, where we had tea, laid on by the Food Flying Squad in the village school.

The exercise brought 'C' Group to a farm incident. People were found in cowsheds and on barn roofs. The local people were our in full force including the Vicar, who wore CD uniform with his collar.

August

Saturday we moved to Luton, where we slept in the Drill Hall. On Sunday morning we moved to Epsom. On route I had a smash but not to worry it was the Policeman's car!

During August I did my first large job as photographer. I went to Swansea with David Creasy to "Sgt" John Pearson's wedding. We reached Swansea at 10.30 and spent the day with John and in the evening we had a little party at the RAFA Club.

Saturday morning dawned bright and sunny. The bridegroom was up with the lark. On route to the Brunswick Methodist Church the taxi driver asked him if he wanted to back out.

"No," said John. "Carry on with the good work."

I took up my post outside the church and took photographs as people arrived. Then I went into the church and sat with David throughout the service. I took groups and close ups outside on the steps and later I took a few at the wedding breakfast.

At 2pm we set off for Torquay with John and Barbara in the back. I left them at 11.30. They reached Torquay on Sunday morning at 1.30 am. The journey was quite good, apart from a bit of trouble though brake failure!

Tour 5 – 8.9.53

On Sept 2nd we left Epsom on route for Scotland. Only two days beforehand we had returned from a month's leave at home and to find ourselves back on the road again was quite a shock. No doubt that was why we lost one rescue group and later on half of the admin echelon. However, we reached Royston in one column and pitched our tents for a night halt.

At 9am the next day we moved to Lincoln, where we stayed the night in a girls' school. One outstanding feature was Lincoln Cathedral, with its three majestic towers standing high in the sky. We were inspected by the Mayor, who welcomed us to the city. After tea, three double deckers took us to the Civil Defence Club, where we were entertained by the "NIBS" Concert party. It was a very nice party and at the end the Brigadier made a fine little speech in thanks.

Friday we moved onto Norton Fire Station, Sheffield, where we are staying until next Tuesday. On Friday evening we had and exercise in Rotherham. I was in reserve with the floodlights. However, I had a call from Mr Patton, who required lights at the farm he was working on. I went up, put the lights up, started the engine and a flood of light was shed on the incident. Tea was laid on by the WVS before we returned to Norton, where we had hot soup before retiring to bed.

Saturday we did a publicity drive of Sheffield during the morning and ended up with an inspection by his worship the Mayor and the town clerk.

Exercise 'Vulcan'

On Sunday morning we left the camp at 9 am for the RV in Sheffield. I was in reserve group and when the column had been deployed I moved with the QL to Column HQ. Then Mr Booker said he wanted me to go up to the Civil Defence HQ, where the Controller was. We drove under the guidance of three D/Rs who took Maclachan and I through the city and up the hill, away from the grime and buildings and into the country.

We parked the van and Johny France and company laid a telephone line down the drive of this big house, around the house and into the garden, past flowerbeds, down some steps and along a terrace. Then a doorway, which led back under the flowerbeds, revealed a twisting passage that led me into the control room.

There were some young ladies working a telephone switchboard and covering a wall was a map of Sheffield. Various officers sat at desks, some writing, others were changing 'tabs' on a tab board that showed where every AMB, REV, VCH, etc, was deployed.

Everything was well under control. We were not kept very busy. Just a few situation reports and a few requests for more rescue parties. We returned to Norton for dinner.

Monday and today we are working on our vans and going out during the afternoon. Tomorrow we move to Carlisle. On Monday morning we went to Wakefield, where we visited the National Coal Board rescue training centre. We were taken through the range, which was just like being in a coalmine. Then they gave us a demonstration with the range full of smoke. They went in with breathing equipment on and brought out a man who had been trapped by a roof fall. They were gone about six minutes.

Our trip to Carlisle was quite a long one, some 160 miles. This was followed by a guard and the following day we moved onto Hawick. We are now in Scotland. We drove through hills purple with heather. Sheep wandered over hill and dale and by the roadside, through the valleys and over tumbling streams which splash their way down the ravine over the rocks, bordered on both side by trees which are now beginning to change colour.

From Hawick we moved to Edinburgh, where we were to stay at Springwell House, quite near to the city centre, the date now being Sept 11th. We arrived during the Festival. During the afternoon we went on a publicity tour of the city with a salute in Princes Street. At 8pm in the evening we went by bus to the castle to see the Tattoo. It was a wonderful sight, the castle floodlit with the pipe bands marching up and down on the forecourt. It lasted two hours. The WRA Corps gave a display of club dancing with their own band playing for them. Drill without any command, highland dancing. Then some fun when Rob Roy raided the castle; guns and canons, swordfights and war cries won them an entry to the castle. One sentry on watch on the battlements was attacked by Roy and thrown to his doom in the depths below.

A team of English and Scots army motor mechanics raced each other in the assembly of a Jeep. The winners took just 1 minute and 12 seconds to do it, including driving it up, flashing the lights and sounding the horn! The mass bands played the "Trumpet Voluntary".

Most impressive of all was the "lights out". A solitary piper, way up on the highest point of the castle, played his pipes. We could just catch the sound of it when the wind carried it down. And as he played the lights went out one by one.

Last of all came everyone for the final salute with the bands of the WRAC and the Scots Guards.

Saturday morning we crossed the Forth in the ferry and went on a publicity drive to quite a nice little town by the sea.

Sunday was an 'all groups turnout' to an exercise in Edinburgh, but before the rescue was very well under way a Fire Storm developed and we had to withdraw sharpish. Tea was laid on by the WVS.

Monday was a rest day, so I spent the day touring Edinburgh. I visited the castle where I saw the "Crown of Scotland", the room where Mary Queen of Scots gave birth to James 1st, and a room full of details and exhibits all about the Royal Flying Corps and the RAF.

I had tea and returned to Springwell House to "titivate" myself up to go to the Police dinner and ball laid on in our honour. It was a nice do with all nice things laid on – including young ladies!

17.9.53

We moved from Edinburgh via Falkirk to Glasgow on Tuesday, where we are staying at an RAF station just outside the city.

Yesterday we had an exercise during the morning around the docks. We loaded all the rescue kit on a launch and went up the Clyde about half a mile to a liner the SS *Circassia*. I had a walkie-talkie as a link back to Mr Booker, who relayed back to CDL for the Column Commander. We climbed aboard by using a rope ladder about 40 feet long; it seemed quite a climb. Six people were trapped and suffering from crush injuries. The boys of 'C' Group soon had them out and lowered into our launch. On the return journey back to the vans we were served with sandwiches and biscuits and hot coffee.

The afternoon was quiet but the evening brought another call for 'C' Group. It was in a steel work factory but nothing out of the ordinary. One report I sent stated that parties were usefully employed. We ended up at the car park, which was full of LA Rescue Vehicles, Ambulances, fire engines and police cars. The intention was to work out a parking plans should mobile columns ever come to work in Glasgow. The Food Flying Squad provided hot pies and tea.

We reached base at about 11pm, with only one idea in mind. Bed!

25.9.53

We are now at RAF Long Benton, near Newcastle. On our last day at Glasgow we went to Calderbridge, where we had an afternoon exercise with not outstanding features. That was Sunday. On Monday we did a road move to Dumfries. On route there were inspections at Coatbridge and Hamilton. It rained all day so we were not very pleased when we found we were sleeping in an RAF hangar. However, after tea Mr Whit and I, with the Humber seats as pillows, bedded down for the night.

On Tuesday I was on advance party again, on the journey to Newcastle. We had quite a good journey down; at one time I was doing 70 mph as we went over a hump as members of the RAF stood to and flew.

Wednesday we spent cleaning up and getting the wagons spick and span. Yesterday we went on a publicity drive to Tynemouth, Whitley Bay and neighbouring towns. We ended up with a tip-top exercise on a Civil Defence and Fire Service Training Ground, where we worked with sirens, the bangs, gas, and live wires. Tea and pies were served after the all clear.

Today we are at Exercise "Irbea" in Newcastle. It is night-time. On arrival there were two terrific explosions in the large petrol store. There has been H.E. bombing on three bases and we have the task of cleaning all three. Ambulances are short and holding works up. Mr Brown went to Dockland by launch with a rescue party to rescue a trapped crew on a ship which has been hit. The exercise ended before time. We always seem to manage to beat the clock before returning to base.

NOTE: Speedo reading today was 35,072, thus making a total of 5,000 miles to date.

From Newcastle we moved to Rufford Abbey via Easingwold, where we had a rest day before a 185 mile run right through to Epsom. During the Scottish tour I covered 1675 miles. Now for a few days leave!

8.11.53

I have let this slip a long time but I am going to recall as much of the past month as I can.

PRIVATE NOTE: While we were in South Wales my 21st birthday came along. I was invited to stay with the Pearsons at Swansea, so I went. At breakfast I received my mail and some very nice gifts from my host and hostess. We then went a car ride to Gower Bay before lunch. We went to Barbara's for tea and had wedding cake. In the evening we went to church. A quiet and happy day. Just what I had always hoped for.

Tour 6

Nearly every time we have a bad start and today it was another wet start. However for a change we are going south from Epsom. Our journey took us down to Compton Bassett for a night halt before proceeding to Falfield, which was to be our base for the first half of the Tour.

Our first job in the southern region was a publicity drive to Bristol, where we were inspected by the Mayor. Being a "local" man I was introduced to his worship.

The drive continued – one half to Weston and the other to Portishead and Clevedon. After tea it was a race to see which group would be back into Bristol and on the Falfield road.

The tour continued with visits to Swansea, Newport and Cardiff before returning to Epsom.

Tour 8

We drove down to Taunton via Shepton Mallet and down to Plymouth where we were passed at Tamerton Folist and had to generate our own lights and heat our water in buckets on the little stoves. We had a trip down to Bodmin. Then we journeyed back to Bournemouth via Exeter. We had a few exercises in Bournemouth before returning Epsom via Winchester. Here the column cam unstuck and went in one way in one and came out in two halves.

Following this came a quick trip to Coventry and Birmingham.

On Dec 5th The Mobile Column went to London and paraded on the Horse Guards Parade with the Mobile Fire Column. The salute was taken by the Home Secretary, Marshal Douglas Hollis, who came and spoke to me while the column was open to the public.

During the next fortnight, little trips were made in the London Area, using Woolwich Barracks as a base, but I was absent from the trips and back at Epsom, in bed, being nursed by the EMC Matron.

At the camp on Dec 17th it was like Christmas Day. Sergeants brought tea to us while we were in bed. Breakfast was at 9am and was followed by a comic relay race. At 1pm came lunch, and what a lunch! The chef served it up as well as it would be obtained at the Ritz. This was followed with smokes, drinks, chocs and nuts. The afternoon … sleep.

At 8 pm, life started again with a dance, plenty of pretty young girls, a band and dainty refreshments made for a most enjoyable evening.

After Christmas everyone packed and left Epsom on January 1st, but seven men left knowing they would return within a month, and I was one of them. Roll on, oh happy day!

Out with 1953 … in with 1954.

On Jan 27th "the seven" returned to Epsom late in the afternoon. A meal was served to us in the kitchen and we were soon quite at home. The next few days were spent doing little jobs about the camp. Then came Monday Feb 1st. At 7.30am Lieutenant Brown and I left in a PCV for the station. The world was white and it was very cold. It took 12 hours before they all arrived so John Carter, Paddy Costello, Len Fox and I were very glad to get to bed.

During the next few days the "new boys" were kitted out and told which group they were going into. I found 12 very nice chaps were to form the new Signals Section and soon got to know them. On the 9th Feb training started and Sigs found themselves doing first aid and basic rescue for a fortnight.

"The 7" were use as assistant instructors and had quite a good time. This was followed by a hard time for me. Sergeant Price and Lieutenant Patton went off to Aldershot to train the DRs to ride motorbikes. That left A/C Chivers in charge. Mr Booker used to make out a programme and I used to take the boys out and get them clued up! When the DRs returned we used to go out on joint exercises.

We used to do some very nice trips such as going to Windsor and on around to NW London Working Radio and Testing Range. We made good contact once from HQFC at Stanmore direct to Epsom, a good 30 miles. On other days we used to go down to the coast.

Column training now over two trail runs to Pirbright were made. On return from the first, a big mess-up was caused by the Column on a roundabout and on the second we had to fight a bush fire at Pirbright. Both runs were quite good and everyone got an idea of what life on the Column is really like.

This year we have no QL but instead we have what is called a Mobile Sector Control (MSC). It is made up of two vans – my 202 and 430. Mine is the Comms HQ and the other is the Sector Controller's office. I had the pleasure of taking these two vans to the Home Office one afternoon for show and from there they went on show to the L.C.C. (I certainly meet the people!).

At the big Epsom Exercise before going on tour the MSC was used. Mr Evans was sector controller and I was his staff officer. The boys manned the radio and telephone exchange and everything seemed to work quite well, so roll on the tours, lets get mobile!

P.S. A/C1 Chivers is now Corporal Chivers. The first time he went out with "them" up was when in best CD at the Home Office. The remark he was greeted with by a passer-by was, "Cor, stone the crows, a corporal in the CD!"

Tour 1 – 11.5.54

On 5th May we left Epsom in bright sunshine at 9 am for our first tour.

We had a flypast the mayor of Reigate at about 50mph. By the time we reached Maidstone we had got into the swing of convoy driving and crawled up the High Street at 5mph, giving everyone a good chance to see us. All would have been well, but a milk lorry ran into one of the Admin lorries and milk was spilled in front of the civic gentlemen.

We had a good lunch by the roadside, 202 being an all-round dining room.

After lunch we moved on to Canterbury, where – 3rd time lucky – we had a good drive past the Mayor before entering our base. After tea we went to the Marlowe Theatre and saw *The Green Pack* – a very nice play. We were the guests of the city. We had a walk around the city before returning to base at 11 pm.

Thursday and Friday we were free during the day with exercises during the evenings. The Mobile Sector Control has not come into being yet, but 202 has spent both evenings in the car park outside Canterbury CD HQ.

On Saturday the Column left Canterbury and moved to Hastings, where we were having lunch cooked by the WVS. On the way we had tea and buns at Tenterdon, after an inspection. At Hastings we had lunch sitting at tables on the prom. Crowds of people stood and watched us. The lunch was very fair but could have been better. We moved on at 2pm to Eastbourne, where we were again inspected and given a very nice tea in the Winter Gardens.

Sigs and DRs were to sleep in a Church Hall. This we found 100 yards from the sea, with a gas boiler that provided hot water for shaving. From 6pm we were free. Well, there was the sea, the coloured lights and the smell of fresh sea air mingled with the scent of wallflowers and RAF boys on the prom looking at the tulips, having a good time. Some mothers won't get their son's hankies to wash next weekend!

Sunday morning we were at home to the public with the Eastbourne town band in attendance. Mr Evans was seen conducting the latter with an expert touch.

Signals staff spent half an hour showing three girls around and showing them the MSC. In the afternoon the girls were seen walking again with signals staff towards Beachy Head!

During the evening "The Casanova Twins" Chivers and Taylor were walking on the prom with a girl on each arm. They were nice girls from the Methodist Church, so we had quite a nice time at Eastbourne!

On Monday we left Eastbourne at 8am and climbed over the downs towards Brighton. We stopped just outside Peacehaven. It was a wonderful morning. The sea was a delightful blue, sun was shining and the air was so fresh as we laid on the cliff, enjoying it all. Then we moved to Brighton and Hove, where we were inspected by the Mayor. Coffee and biscuits were provided. Then on along the coast to Worthing, where again we had an inspection and a nice lunch cooked by the WVS. This time we sat in private inside an open-air concert hall on the prom. After lunch everyone had the same idea… Trousers rolled up and into the sea went all the boys! It was very nice after all of Sundays walking.

From Worthing we moved to Littlehampton and on to RAF Tangmere, which is only 7 miles from the sea, so we still have nice fresh air. Our tour ended with the run back to Epsom along the London road to Dorking, where we picked up the road for Epsom. We reached base, had lunch and started washing and cleaning the vans ready for Tour 2.

During this short tour we had a very nice time. Good bases, food and weather and always hot water. I fear some of the new people will have gathered a wrong impression of life on the Column!

We had some very local support on different occasions during the past week. One old man stood to attention and saluted while the column passed him before he moved. At another place a woman all on her own in CD uniform clicked her heels and saluted every van, lorry and motorbike as it passed her. It seemed funny to us, but it proved in what esteem they held us.

4.   A Years' Detachment with EMC 1954

by Jim Carson (2599924 A/C Carson, J., Royal Air Force)

It must be understood by all readers that these notes were written in often abominably bad conditions. No responsibility is therefore assumed for bad or illegible writing, although I have done my utmost to avoid such at all times. I sincerely hope, that you, the reader, will find my notes interesting.

Introduction

As all the adventures depicted herein were experienced during my National Service, I will start by a short description of events leading up to my detachment to the Mobile Column.

Joining the RAF on 24th July 1953, I reported to Cardington, Bedfordshire, where, after being kitted out and generally accepted into the service, I was posted to Hednesford in Staffordshire for two months of recruit training. From there to my permanent unit – RAF Sandwich, Kent – where I had 12 weeks training as a clerk accounts, passing my trade test in January 1954. While there, I applied to serve on the Column for one year, little thinking that I would be accepted!

But one day I was told that I had indeed been accepted and so, on February 1st in the year 1954, I and another one hundred and nineteen airmen arrived at Epsom in Surrey, wondering just what they had let themselves in for …

Training

The Mobile Column at Epsom, Surrey is quite a unique depot, being the only unit in Great Britain where Army and Royal Air Force Personnel work and live together and receive instruction from civilians. Approximately fifty men of the Royal Artillery arrived with the airmen and these men trained for all of three months, as Civil Defence Workers, being paid by the Home Office at service rates.

We trained in all aspects of rescue work, reconnaissance and first aid. Driving instruction was given by the London Passenger Transport Driving School, Chiswick and the Despatch Rider Section was trained at the Royal Corps or Military Police Barracks, Woking. The three rescue units (hereafter A, B, and C,) trained on the special training ground on the unit itself, and signals section also were unit trained.

This training continued through March and April and on the fifth day of May, the first tour of the No. 1. Mobile Column, Civil Defence Corps, commenced.

Tour 1 – Kent and Sussex

Wednesday, May 5

We moved out of the CD depot, Epsom at 09.30 hours and proceeded towards Reigate via Banstead. At Reigate, the Mayor and other civic heads, including the Superintendent of Surrey Police and Chief Fire Officer of East Surrey, took the salute at the Town Hall as the Column drove past.

Lunch was provided near Harrietsham by our mobile kitchen vans and then onto the county town of Kent, Maidstone, where another drive past took place at the Town Hall, in the extremely busy High Street. However, police control was good and the column got through in two echelons. There was a minor accident opposite the saluting base when a rescue stores van collided with a milk lorry.

At Canterbury there was another full drive past at Lady Wootton's Green, close

to the ruins of the town walls, and the Mayor was again in attendance to take the salute. After that, the Column moved to Wemyss Barracks, a training camp of the Home Counties Brigades, where we were billeted in the former stables.

In the evening, column personnel were entertained at the Marlowe Theatre by the Canterbury Theatre Company showing *The Green Pack* by Edgar Wallace. A most enjoyable show.

Thursday, May 6

A day of general preparation and maintenance in the barracks. In the evening, commencing 17.00 hours, the column took part in Exercise "Spread-eagle" at the three points, Margate, Dover and Sittingbourne. At each of these places, a full-scale rescue exercise in conjunction with local forces was carried out and the local forces emergency feeding centres then had their exercises, which were fully enjoyed by all concerned. Mobile first aid units and National Hospital Reserve Forces were also in attendance. In the Town Hall, Dover, "C" Unit were given a warm welcome by the Mayor as they had their late meal, before returning to base at Canterbury.

Friday, May 7 – "Exercise Mobcol"

Another evening exercise, at three points: Herne Bay, Whitstable and Canterbury. Not so much rescue work this time, but emergency feeding centres in operation in all areas, and a great many interested onlookers at each incident. The visit of the Experimental Mobile Column to East Kent has given the local CD divisions a great idea of what is required, and also some practice of work with a mobile rescue column.

Saturday, May 8

An early start leaves Canterbury behind and we move on up the A259 through Ashford to Tenterden, where there is a drive past the deputy mayor and civic heads. In the local public park, Ashford division WVS provided a teabreak with cakes, then on through Northiam and Brede to Hastings, where a great show was laid on to herald the visit of EMC 1954.

In Warrior Square, opposite the seafront, the column and personnel lined up and were inspected by the Lord Mayor. Following this, the column personnel were fed by an emergency meals mobile centre formed on the beach. Luckily, the weather was fine and many early summer holidaymakers watched the 220 men eat an enjoyable meal beside the mobile centre.

At 13.45 hours, the Lord Mayor took the salute on the Hastings boundary and we moved on along the coast road, through St Leonard's-on-Sea.

At Bexhill, the Mayor, along with the EMC Commandant, Brigadier D.A.L. Mackenzie CBE, DSO, took the salute at the 5 m.p.h. drive past.

Arriving Eastbourne at 15.00 hours, the column formed up the review order on Devonshire Place, where the Mayor and the Deputy Mayor inspected vehicles and men. This inspection took longer than expected, as the 70-year-old Mayor had a word to say to each man of the EMC. Then, in three flights, personnel marched to the Winter Gardens, where tea was provided by the local authorities.

At 17.00 hours for one hour, vehicles were open for public inspection in Devonshire Place.

At 18.30 Column moves to quarters.

Of the first tour, the quarters at Eastbourne were the worst. The vehicles and mobile kitchens were situated in the grounds of a disused Sussex Light Infantry Barracks. "A" Unit were billeted in Ashfern Street RC School, "B" Unit in a garage, "C" Unit in a barn converted into sleeping quarters, and the Communications Section in Christ Church Mission Hall, Firle Street.

Straw palliasses were used.

Sunday, May 9

Rest day. Vehicles open to public inspection 11 a.m. – 12 noon, with the Eastbourne Town Brass Band providing music. Free for the rest of the day, we viewed Eastbourne's tulips.

Monday, May 10

Five a.m. Reveille for an early start to Worthing and today was the hottest day so far in 1954, with a temperature of 79 degrees. A great number of us agreed that our run along the beautiful South Coast was one of the finest we had had. Good practice for the Scottish tour was gained on numerous steep hills on the A259 out of Eastbourne.

Our first inspection was on the Brighton/Hove boundary where the mayors of these two towns had a look at us before letting us loose on a small mobile café which served us a free and excellent break. Then we were mobile again along the coast road, through Southwick, Seaford, Newhaven, and Shoreham-by-Sea.

In Worthing the column lined up in review order and Column and personnel were inspected by the mayor and civic officials, after which the mayor gave an address of welcome on behalf of the townspeople to EMC 1954.

Then followed a meal in the beach pavilion by the WVS and for the ninth time in five days we had stew! Dear me! The stew issue is becoming rather a problem and I hear that the Commandant had complained to the WVS feeding centres about it.

We had some free time in Worthing and this was appreciated by all of us who wanted to view the local "sights". At 2pm we were off again and on our run to RAF Tangmere, where we were billeted for two evenings. We passed through some lovely countryside.

At Littlehampton, the C.O., Sqn/Ldr Dobbing, viewed the column from the cockpit of a Cutlass monoplane. Another place we passed through was Arundel, with its mighty castle, seat of the Duke of Norfolk, and then on to Tangmere, a large fighter command jet station, situated three miles from Chichester.

The run from Worthing was not only notable for its beauty, but also for the number of local wardens and Civil Defence Corps Personnel, who stood solemnly at the roadside and whipped up a smart and sincere salute as the column drove by. One particularly energetic female warden clicked her heels and saluted each wagon in quick succession, as the column went on.

The move was successful apart from three punctures and the removal of a Surrey County Council manhole cover by a CRV en route.

Tuesday, May 11

A morning of maintenance and an afternoon of sunbathing. Exercise "Regforce" in the evening in Chichester, an exercise of deployment to the local civil defence volunteers to give them practice at handling the arrival of a mobile column. RV was at the famous Goodwood Racecourse.

Wednesday, May 12

This, our last day of Tour 1, was spent on the return 54-mile journey from RAF Tangmere to Epsom. The route took us through some beautiful Sussex countryside, and villages like Duncton,

Petworth, and Northchapel. At Haslemere, we had an inspection by the Mayor and Chairman of the UDC, but in the boiling sunshine, a parade was the last thing we wanted.

From Haselmere, into Surrey and Godalming and Guildford back to Epsom via the route we know so well.

So that is Tour 1 over and we unanimously agree that it has been an enjoyable one. I have enjoyed every bit of it and have seen some very interesting new places. The weather on the tour has been excellent with the hottest day of the year last Tuesday.

Tour 2 – East Anglia and Midlands

On Tuesday 18th May, the column pulled out of Epsom at the crack of dawn, on the first stage of Tour Two, to Warley Barracks, Brentwood, Essex. En route, the column had its first real experience of getting lost, because on some parts of the North Circular Road there were as many as six or seven small columns, some even travelling in opposite directions!

I didn't leave Epsom until the following day, when I drove the Commandant to Southend-on-Sea, where we rejoined the main column on exercise there.

The exercise went off fairly well, with incidents on the Southend gasworks pier, a sewage farm, Leigh-on-Sea railway station and at Shoeburyness. The emergency feeding exercise following was not a success.

Thursday, May 20th – "Mobco"

Maintenance during the day and Exercise "Mobco" in the evening at Romford and Hornchurch. Gas was used in the Hornchurch incidents and this hampered the rescuers until torrential rain came and cleared the air. This fact, however, had to be pointed our to the CDO, for had he had his way, the rescue parties would have been toiling in respirators in the downpour for long enough.

"A" Unit also suffered in the following feeding exercise, the local authorities having less idea than the CDO of what was required for a tired and hungry rescue unit.

Saturday, May 22nd

As Friday was a rest day, there is nothing more to say, but today, the Column had one of its biggest "jobs" yet, Exercise "Tilbury" at Tilbury Docks. This was expected to be the cat's whiskers of exercises, but it didn't turn out altogether that way.

An "A" bomb had burst over the dock at 2,000 feet and local forces, including an auxiliary fire column, were rushed in, but were unable to cope, so the Mobile Column was sent for.

There were hitches, of course, when one rescue party was held up in its work to let the new P&O liner *Arcardia* pass downstream.

Following the exercise the Eastern Convoy of the Food Flying Squad provided us with hot soup and sandwiches. This was our first meeting with the F.F.S., but we all hope to see much more of them on tour this year, because the grub we get from them is of a very high standard. Their brilliant blue vans and cookers are always a very welcome sight to all in the E.M.C.

Sunday, May 23rd – Exercise "Askey"

We had an early start from base a Warley, but a lovely run through Essex and Herts to Bedfordshire, where "Askey" was taking place at Luton.

En route the column had lunch on Harpenden Common, provided by our mobile kitchens, although a certain few of the boys were put off their food by the timely arrival of three French girl cyclists!

By the time the column was deployed to the incidents it was 1500 hours and a large crowd of spectators had formed at the Luton Airport incident, where "A" and "B" units were hard at it. Along with local forces, volunteers from Vauxhall Motors and Percival Aircraft Factories were also working and the exercise was a success, ending with tea in the workers canteen in the airport.

Leaving Luton at 18.20 hours, the return journey was made in good weather, via Hertford, St Albans, Harpenden and Hatfield, to arrive at base 20.00 hours.

Monday, May 24

Rest and maintenance.

Tuesday, May 25

After spending the last seven nights at the depot of the Essex Regiment, the Column moved north on the run to Norwich. We made good time through Chelmsford and Colchester to Ipswich, where the first drive past of the day took place. The salute was taken by the Chairman of the CD committee and Brigadier McKenzie, Commandant of the EMC.

At Woodbridge, lunch was by our own kitchens, and then at Lowestoft the newly-elected Mayor inspected the first six vehicles of the Column, following which he took the salute at a drive past.

The third and last drive past was in the market square, Great Yarmouth, where on the saluting dais, surrounded by fish boxes and fish-and-chip shops, were the Mayor, Brigadier McKenzie and other civic heads. Following this, we were given cold, weak, tea and rock buns by ladies of the WVS.

Then Norwich, here we come… We arrived in brilliant sunshine to find ourselves billeted in Brittania Barracks, depot of the Royal Norfolk Regiment, and Nelson Barracks, a disused TA depot. That doesn't sound too bad, but as they were about a mile apart by road and with one at the top of a miniature mountain, it wasn't so grand, and there was "much wailing and gnashing of teeth"

Wednesday, May 26

At 3pm in the square adjoining the City Hall, Norwich, vehicles and personnel were inspected by the deputy mayoress. It was one of the biggest inspections we have had so far, but all was well. There was a big attendance of local CD heads and WVS personnel, while the public provided a huge gallery at each end of the street.

Exercise 'Mobcol'

A fairly large exercise was held in the evening at various incidents in the city. Our mobile sector control vans, the only vehicles of their kind in existence, were in use.

Thursday, May 27

The longest run of EMC 1954 to date took place when the Column moved from Norwich through six English counties to Ecceshall. The six counties were Norfolk, Lincolnshire, Leicestershire, Nottinghamshire, Derbyshire and into Staffs, and the mileage was from 175-200 miles. The first incident was a drive past at Kings Lynn, taken by the mayor and the MT staff had their first headache when an FD van broke down just after saluting the dais.

Between there and Holbeach a second vehicle broke down and by the time we halted for lunch there was a smaller CD column about half an hour behind the main column, made up of MT vehicles and "casualties". A very fine lunch was provided in the Women's Institute,

Holbeach by the WVS and we were soon off again through Grantham to the next halt at Bottesford, an emergency refuelling point.

On the banks of the river Trent, in Nottingham we me the North Midlands Food Flying Squad and were provided with another good meal, up to the very high standard of all these blue vans which we have learned to look to as the kings of mobile feeding. Manned by the WVS, the excellent service provided cannot be too highly praised.

Before reaching Derby we encountered a severe hailstorm and in the torrents lost part of the MT section and also the Land Rover of "A" Unit.

These were immediately enrolled as members to the Grant Map Reading courses[2] and later rejoined the column by different routes! The day was ended by the disappearance of a D/R and his cycle into a six-foot ditch, and the loss of the MT towing wagon in Slone, up a very narrow side-road.

We are accommodated at the Drakes Hall Hostel near Eccleshall for the next

---

[2] A course formed by the officers of E.M.C., in name of the catering officer, "Jock" Giant who always gets lost on even the shortest route. "NEVER" in the field of mobile columns, has so little got lost so many times, in such a short distance.

seven nights. This hostel, disused for seven years, was a women's training college, now owned by the Ministry of Works. Easily the best accommodation we have had had on the tours this year, and some say, "I wish Epsom depot was like this!"

Friday, May 28 – Exercise "Gothic"

Only two units were required for this exercise, the first in Stoke-on-Trent area for five years.

"C" Unit was at the disused pottery, Newport Lane, Burslem, but the situation there was soon out of hand when a real fire broke out. Soon fire brigades from all around were rushing to the scene and what was once a CD exercise became a blazing inferno. The volunteer casualties became real life-or-death ones, but with the help of a good supply of water the fire services managed to put out the blaze and frantic officials could mop their brows and breathe sighs of relief.

On exercise with the Mobile Column, were large contingents of local volunteers in ambulance and police sections.

To crown the evening's excitement, the police guide car led the column underneath a 9ft 9in railway bridge. Luckily the leading CRV halted in time, but much chaos followed when all 12 vehicles had to do almost an about-turn in the narrow, busy street. That alone upset the Stoke traffic for the remainder of the evening.

Sunday May 30th – Exercise "Priory"

Yesterday was a rest day and preparation for the activities of today. Our visit to Coventry has long been the talk in many circles, as you will have seen from the newspapers. Coventry disbanded its CD Committee a few months ago and proclaimed that it really wasn't interested in Civil Defence any longer, so on the result of our visit will depend the future of this vital work in one of the premier cities of the Midlands. To quote from the *Daily Mirror* of 29/5/54:- "Coventry, the city that decided to distance its CD Committee because of the destructive power of the H-bomb, is to have an H-bomb exercise tomorrow. The CD Experimental Mobile Column will visit the city during its tour of the Midland region. Coventry asked for the exercise last November, before the decision to disband."

We did expect a bit of opposition when we arrived at the incidents, but at one particular place, the CD exercise turned into the Battle of Priory Row.

Loudspeaker vans from the rival party led by the six socialist councillors, endeavoured to shout down the exercise commentary, and all the time while casualties were being rescued, these two voices blared at each other from opposite sides of the street. You will perhaps have read of this incident in the national newspapers, but at the time of writing the socialist rebels in Coventry were demanding an interview with the Home Secretary and at the same time demanding the resignation of the Principal Officer of the CD Midland Region.

On the whole, the incident was gross exhibitionism in bad taste. The exercise in other parts of Coventry, for example at Webster's Brickyards, went off fairly well, and the rescue parties met some good problems and dealt with them.

There were large crowds of the general public at each post, owing to the national publicity the exercise had received. It was also the first occasion in which an H-bomb had exploded over the country.

The return run to base was made in heavy rain via Atherstone, Lichfield and Rugby; total mileage 124 miles.

Monday May 31st – Publicity Tour

The first real publicity drive took place over 45 miles in the Potteries area of the Midlands. We called first at Longton and Fenton and then at Hanley, where, on a spare piece of ground above the town, the Lady Mayoress of Stoke-in-Trent inspected us as we lined up beside our vehicles.

The 15 miles-per-hour drive continued through Burslem and Stoke to Newcastle-under-Lyme, where amid a surrounding of factory chimneys and potteries, the Lady Mayoress inspected both Column and personnel. Following this, the publicity tour crawled on its way out of Newcastle, through numerous suburbs and into the open countryside. The weather was fine but the pace of 15mph and 15 yards apart was most exhausting.

Tuesday, June 1st – Shrewsbury

Leaving Eccleshall at 09.30 hours, the column proceeded to Shrewsbury via Newport. There we lined up in the Quarry Park, on the banks of the River Severn, and from 11am until lunchtime the vehicles were open to inspection by the general public. At 1pm the mayor and other civic heads, together with many Army and RAF officers, inspected the vehicles, after which we were free for two hours to see the sights of Shrewsbury – and fairly pleasing some of these sights were!

Boats could be hired on the river at two bob a time, and many had a go at the strenuous sport, having at the same time, some close shaves with racing "sculls" and "eights" at practice from Shrewsbury School.

The return drive to base was made in dull weather to Wolverhampton and, apart from losing the MT officer, a breakdown of part of "C" Unit in busy Stafford and a dangerously low bridge, it was uneventful. Distance 78 miles.

Wednesday, June 2nd – Exercise "Yum Bum Frum" – Dudley

The entire column left base at 5pm for Dudley in North Worcestershire, about ten miles from Birmingham. The place of rendezvous attracted a large crowd of local kids, who clambered all over our vehicles, jabbering in their peculiar Black Country accent, which few could understand.

The exercise was held in an ideal area in the centre of Dudley, where quite a number of streets with derelict houses were in use, but when we arrived it was

found that only one rescue party out of the eighteen on the Column was required, so a large number of the men were idle. Some of the NCOs, after discovering the poor quality of the flying squad tea, retired to the nearby "Green Dragon" for the remainder of the exercise. Much night driving experience was gained on the return run via Wolverhampton and Stafford.

Thursday, June 3rd – Eccleshall to Epsom

Another long run was made by the Column today, a distance of approx 170 miles. Leaving Eccleshall at 9am we had refuelling at Stone and finally pulled out at 10am through Stafford, Rugeley and Lichfield. South of Kenilworth we caught up on our kitchen column, and there partook of our lunch. Then we pushed further south, through Leamington Spa and Banbury to Kidlington, where we had refuelling of two kinds, petrol for our "jalopies" and tea for ourselves.

Then to Watford, where a small MG police car took us on the very complicated by-pass. Of all the guide cars we have had on Tour 2, I think it was easily the best and would have won the prize for the most neat.

Into Middlesex now, through Staines and then over the border into Berkshire, towards Maidenhead. In Maidenhead thicket, the Chief Constable of Berkshire led an inspection party of our vehicles, and that, thank goodness, was the last inspection of Tour 2.

An enjoyable run along the Thames to Hampton Court and then Chessington eventually brought us into Epsom at 9.45pm, and we drove into the depot about two minutes late. The scenery on the last part of the route was most enjoyable, to say the least of it!*

Perhaps the best part of our return to camp was the fact that on Friday we left on the Annual Whitsun grant. We didn't leave Epsom, however, until rather late - just another example of the overall incompetence to organise anything on the part of our military authorities! (Had to get that in!)

June 9-11 1954 – Special Tour, London

Some bright specimen must have got his notes mixed, to land us with a short London Region Tour in between Tours 2 and 3.

On the 9th we did a publicity drive through Cheam, Mitcham and Streatham to Lambeth. In Brockwell Park the mayors of Lambeth and Camberwell inspected us and our vehicles in pouring rain. Our visit rounded off a week of CD exhibitions and recruiting campaigns in the area. In the evening "C" Unit were on exercise in Fulham, while the remainder returned to base by the same route.

The 10th was our Queen's official birthday and in the evening an exercise was held on our training ground for the benefit of local Surrey CD forces. Commencing at 6pm, the Column spent three hours in a car park on call, before doing quite a successful exercise. I had my first session as an ambulance loader, as I wasn't required on my normal task, but I won't say that we didn't have a good time.

The 11th saw us off on a publicity tour of several SE London boroughs, with tea provided by the WVS at Deptford CD centre. After this, the Mayor and Lady Mayoress of Deptford inspected us and for a short time, the public had the opportunity to look around.

Tour 3 – Scotland and North

Part 1 – Tuesday, 15th June 1954

The column pulled out from the Depot at 7.30am and there were signs that not all of the wagons wished to leave, as about 100 yards from the gate, there was the first hold-up, when an Austin with a Sassenach driver, broke down.

But it was a great day for we Scots as the column wound its way round the North Circular road and headed north to bonny Scotland, 300 miles away, reclining in the wondrous heather and beautiful country.

I personally did not move out on this day, but remained behind and made the run to Washington later. The Column's night halt was at Rufford Abbey, Ollerton.

This old abbey, once a mansion house belonging to King Charles II, was, I am sure, one of the eeriest quarters the column has experienced, and it has a very sorry record of love affairs for the then young Romeos, *viz* King Edward VI, who was "chucked out" of the Abbey after one particularly busy evening. However, among cobwebs and dust in ancient banquet halls and perhaps execution chambers, EMC 1954 bedded down.

Wednesday, June 16th

The second day of the long run north to TA camp No.151 WETC, Washington, Sunderland.

I left Epsom today and arrived at Washington only ten minutes behind the main Column from Ollerton, a journey of about 289 miles. An uneventful day.

Thurs June 17th – "Crossing the Border"

The run today was a short one, and only 73 miles from Washington to Hawick. The main thing was that today we were leaving England and into bonnie Scotland, so it was not surprising that the column speed was pretty fast, as column Commander was Lieutenant "Jock" Brown from Glasgow.

Plenty of hilly country gave the drivers valuable gearbox experience and at times the hills spread the column over many miles. Up front, the two Consuls and "A" Unit's Land Rover were alone for quite a time, the larger vehicles making heavy weather of it.

The route was via Corbridge and Otterburn to the actual crossing at Carter Bar. Our Scots Commandant, Brigadier Mackenzie, was in great form as he welcomed each vehicle across, to the tune of a Jimmy Shand reel on our wireless sets. Aye, Aye, it was a great occasion indeed, and when, sixteen miles farther on, we reached Hawick to spend the night, there was rejoicing in the hearts of all true Scots on the Column.

To this date, the meal provided at lunch by Hawick WVS was easily the finest eaten by EMC '54 and a fitting welcome to Scots food.

Two units were billeted in the local school while "C" Unit and Comms Flight made the best of a wooden floor at the TA drill hall. It was not at all surprising that a large number of the chaps slept in their vehicles; one signals chap even finding the three seats of a Land Rover ample to stretch out on.

Friday June 18th 1954

On the 110 miles from Hawick to base at RAF Bishopbriggs, the scenery was beautiful, as was the sole policewoman on the force of Galashiels. In this busy little border town, the provost inspected us, although some people took much convincing that he wasn't a mayor!

Then onwards through Melrose, Selkirk and Peebles to the lovely Blyth Bridge. South of Carnwath, we caught up with our mobile kitchens, who provided lunch.

By this time we met our police escort from Galsgow City Police, a Jaguar Mk.V saloon and a fiercely competent motorcyclist. These guided us to Bishopbriggs via Carluke, Newmains, Newhouse and Airdrie, to a petroling point in Kirkintilloch.

Sat 19th June 1954 – Exercise "Morton"

This exercise took place in Greenock where, in heavy rain, Rescue Units "A" & "B" left base at 11am. Before the exercise, the route given took the form of a publicity tour South through Paisley, Renfrew and Johnstone to Lochwinmoch, and then round the coast road via Skelmortie and Wemyss Bay to the RV, which we reached at 2.30pm.

After deployment, guides took the rescue parties to the various incidents, but by this time, the heavy rains were making conditions very uncomfortable for all concerned.

Across the river Clyde at Rumbarton, "C" Unit were having a hectic afternoon with the exercise there. At one part, a rescue party had to cross the Severn, but so strong was the tidal water, that several attempts had to be given up, until a heavy motor boat came to the rescue.

Sunday, June 20th

General maintenance and rest day.

21st – 27th June – Aberdeen

On Monday, we left Bishopbriggs for the bonnie granite city of Aberdeen, 149 miles North. The route was indeed a beautiful one and the rain managed to stay off to let the doubtful English have a sight at bonnie Scotland.

The first main town was Stirling, the "Gateway to the Highlands" and there we saw the Wallace Monument, high on a hill beside the town, with 365 steps one for every day of the year and in which lies the famous sword of William Wallace.

Then Stirling Castle and the old road bridge, which led us out to Dunblane and Auchterarder and eventually the fair city of Perth. On Tay Street, the mobile kitchens were waiting for us and provided the usual meal in the shade of the North Inch's grand trees.

Close to our emergency re-fuelling point in Bargeddie, we saw the Burnham Woods and Dunsenane Hills of *Macbeth,* Cougar Angus, Forfar, Brechin, Laurenakirk, and Stonehaven to Aberdeen.

Our base was at the Bridge of Don barracks of the Gordon Highlands and we frequently heard the music of the pipes from the regimental band.

On Tuesday we had a rest day and a tour of surrounding beauty spots was organised for those who wished. But most of us preferred to explore the silver city and very favourable impressions were gathered. The city corporation organised a grand ball in the Beach Ballroom for the column and a visiting naval destroyer. Music was provided by Tito Burns and his Band.

The following evening we had a large exercise in the city – "Bon Accord" – and it was Aberdeen's largest ever civil defence operation. My vehicle was used as column commander's car on this occasion and the Commandant took a back seat for a change. An after-exercise conference lasted until half-past midnight, by which time I was thoroughly fed up with 3½ hours of car park waiting.

Thursday was again a rest day and we all agreed that the Scottish half of Tour 3, was very easy-going and fairly enjoyable.

Leaving Aberdeen on Friday morning we returned top Glasgow by a different route. This was to accommodate a public viewing at Dundee, but owing to a mistake somewhere up the line, the main viewing party arrived as we pulled out again towards Perth. Our route took us across Kincardine Bridge and via Kilsyth to Bishopbriggs and base for a further four days.

Saturday and Monday were our rest days and we were treated well by the Corporation who issued free cinema (Rita Hayworth in *Miss Sadie Thomson* at the Gaumont) and dance tickets to all, and free beer to that who wished. On Sunday we had a deployment exercise in the city centre, and owing to a faulty set on CD6, I acted as a radio link thought the operations, at sub-control in Stevenson Street.

The three units, with five engines and ambulances, eventually rendezvoused in Glasgow Green, and then the Mobile Column led a grand parade of 84 vehicles through city streets. First came the seven motorcycles of the column, then 28 operational vehicles with mobile sector control vans. They were followed by 30 ambulances, manned by the volunteer ladies of the National Hospital reserve, and then 26 fire appliances from Lanarkshire. The procession halted at Woodside Crescent, where tea and pies were free for all in the CD Headquarters, after which, the three services split up and the column returned to base.

Tuesday June 29th – Back to Uncivilization

All good things must come to an end, and this was one good thing that I was sorry to see end, the terrible day when the column crossed the Border again!

The city police guided us out of the city via numerous back streets to Uddingston and Bothwell. The methods by which their single motor cyclist can escort a convoy, is a wonder to watch, and from reliable sources, I have heard that the Glasgow police are quite exceptional and easily the best in Britain.

The route was a good one, but unfortunately one of the quickest ways out of the country, via Beatlock, Lockerbie and Gretna Green. At Lockerbie, four very enthusiastic civilians took the salute as we drove through but the narrow streets prevented an "eyes right."

And as we crossed the border, half a mile below Gretna our very co-operative record player provided "MacCrimmon's Lament." A sad, sad day! O woe is me! It's not worth saying much about the scenery south of the border – there is none – but for the record we went via Haltwhistle and Corbridge, back to our base for Part 2 - Washington.

Part 2

We were to learn that the Part 2 of the Northern tour was a very busy one, unlike the Scottish half, and perhaps that was the reason for the ease north of the border. Based at the No. 151 WETC, we did six exercises all told, the first being at Jarrow on Wednesday 30th June.

Exercise "Progress" brought into use various industrial CD rescue teams, who worked well with the column parties at the incidents.

Thursday July 1st 1954 – "Mobcol"

This operation took place in the dockland of Sunderland and there were some good problems for all concerned, one being the rescue of two casualties from the floor of a deep dry dock, by means of a very slippery vertical side. Some "enemy casualties" also had to be rescued from the top of a 90-foot church tower, by means of a two-point suspension from that height.

In our Mobile Sector Control there was a considerable confusion over callsigns and Corporal "Dave" Chivers wisely left the operating to an attractive piece from Sunderland division HQ. Not only did her milk-and-honey voice prompt our lads to send in reports twice as fast as

usual, but Corporal Chivers was so overpowered by her competence that he returned half-way to base before he realised she was still close to him.

Friday, July 2nd, 1954 Exercise "Fit"

The third full-scale exercise in three days took place in the Billingham and Stockton areas. We left base at 11.00 hours and headed due south-east through the coalmines and slagheaps of County Durham and its mining towns and villages, to Wolviston, on the outskirts of Billingham, where at the RV we had lunch from the mobile advance kitchens.

At 14.00 hours the exercise commenced with the main incident in the 1320 areas of the I.C.I. works. Other incidents were at the Furness Shipbuilding Yards, and British Titan Products Ltd. Nearly all the problems were of an unusual nature, and the I.C.I. works were an excellent place to practice these, but too often were the tasks set too hopeless to tackle in the time allotted.

Following the exercise, the works entertained all the CD workers to a good tea in their modern staff cafeterias. At Billingham, speeches were made by the Managing Director of I.C.I. Ltd., Brigadier Mackenzie and Mr Hutchinson, the Principal Officer for the

Northern Region. Following this, the column rendezvoused and returned to base.

At this stage I left the Column and returned to Epsom, as my "chief" had an important conference to attend in London. So, on Saturday 3rd July, I left Column base at Washington and made my way to Epsom, via the Brigadier's home at Camberley. The milometer reading was 324 miles, which, after several calculations, I reckon I did an average of 36.7mph and 29.8mpg.

Meanwhile, the column did three exercises at Gateshead, Wallsend and South Shields, and had two rest days before making the two days run back to the depot, which they reached 2¾ hours late on Friday 9th July.

The tour had a fairly heavy accident list and there were numerous minor "prangs". Most serious injury fell on D/R Fred Holmes, who sustained a fracture of the lower thigh in Consett, Co Durham when he "came off" in a collision with a car and a telephone pole.

On the same day, Johnny Christmas managed to convert his Austin Sector control van into a plough, when he "forcibly entered" and churned up a dear old Durham lady's flower garden. Brake failure…

Near Stonehaven, "Chippy" Gray succeeded in scraping a long groove in the side of a Ford Anglia, before putting his BSA through a wire fence. The Ford owner decided not to take any action … until he sent the bill to EMC a few weeks later. Another D/R, Charlie Embling, parted company with his bike after losing an argument with a sharp bend.

In the heavier vehicles, two office vehicles had a tussle with BRS lorries, the column vans receiving cuts and abrasions on their offsides, while nearing Aberdeen, four admin wagons became so friendly as to run into each other when the first braked sharply. Lashings of twisted metal and splintered wood!

If the weather had been a little better I am sure the English chaps would have enjoyed bonnie Scotland more, but the whole tour, especially Part I, was most successful.

However, it was useful in that it gave them just a glimpse of the beauties to be found in this wonderful land – the finest country in the world!

Wednesday, 14th July 1954 – Epsom

I hear there was considerable hard feeling expressed last year when the Column toured all round the UK but did not officially visit its home town of Epsom, so at 11.15am we were formed up in our units in the Baths Hall Car Park, the three rescue units, all HQ vehicles and a selection from the Admin Section, including a kitchen van. The Mayor then inspected us and left for the saluting dais beside the clock tower in the High Street. A few minutes later we moved out of the park into East Street and at 5mph proceeded into High Street, round the top roundabout and back past the saluting dais, and from there back to the depot.

A total of 32 vehicles and seven motor cycles took part and this convoy was sufficient to upset all traffic control through Epsom for the remainder of the day!

16-28 July 1954 – Tour 4 – NW England

On a beautiful summer morning, the 16th July, after a very short stay at the depot, the Column pulled out on Tour 4 with the first night halt again at Rufford Abbey, Ollerton, 142 miles away.

This unwelcoming building, where we have spent quite a few nights this year, held some bad memories for certain of our number. On the 17th, the journey continued in a northern and westerly direction up the A1 to Ferrybridge, then over Ilkley Moor to Skipton and Settle, finally arriving at an Air Cadet training camp near Barrow-in-Furness.

The following three days followed the usual pattern of an exercise on the 18th, Rest Day on the 19th and maintenance on the 20th.

The amount of maintenance spent on column vehicles, in our opinion, is far too much and I personally am quite sure there would be less trouble of a trifling nature, if we were not subjected to so much maintenance periods.

Is it fair? Allegations wholesale

At this stage of our travels, the four military officers became exceedingly unpopular as a result of certain happenings. I might add that this was not the first time by any means when complaints of a serious nature have been levelled at our superiors.

The four, Squadron Leader Dobbing RAF, Flight Lieutenants Birch and Bone of the RAF Regt, and Lieutenant Brown

RE, have, in the opinion of a heavy majority of the EMC personnel, been found guilty of sufficient acts against fellow humans to make these men no longer 'associates'.

Examples were plentiful on Tour 4, during frequent billet inspections, and Flight Lieutenant Bone especially, showed little 'C.S.' Lieutenant Brown was recommended to mercy.

July 21st 1954

Continuing, the Column moved south to the second and last port of call on Tour 4, the Seaforth Barracks, Bootle. Accommodation there was only fair but the surrounding district was found to be of much interest, in many ways!

Before the weekend, two larger exercises were held, the first being at Stockport on the 22nd. The second, on Saturday, was at Chester, where an exceedingly enthusiastic local corps was in action.

At this stage, I rejoined the Column at Seaforth Barracks, having completed the 228-mile run from Epsom in a little under seven hours. The A5 was the road used to Cannock and thereafter the A34/A50 to Queens Drive, Liverpool.

Sunday July 25th

Another exercise, this time in the areas around Birkenhead. Units were also at Wirral and Hoylake. Tea following the exercise was served by the Food Flying Squad (NW Convoy).

Monday, 26th

A rest day, but I managed to be fully occupied driving the Deputy Commandant on a post-exercise conference around Cheshire. Chester was visited twice and Great Crosby once.

Tuesday 28th July 1954

This day went down in the records as being the longest run ever attempted by the Column since its formation. The result was a great success and the 230 miles were covered in good time.

Column Commander was Mr Newman in GYR 882 and he kept good movement, but I am sure that the eventual success of the record run was made possible by the drivers of the leading two vehicles, who adopted a plan to gain one hour in time between lunch at Coleshill and tea at Oxford.

This plan came off, thanks to our two friends, and the column came down the road into base at 21.37 hours.

What a favourable result compared to the drastic closing run of Tour 3!

The route was a well-known one south of Stone as we returned to base that way from Tour 2. Seaforth, Prescot, Warrington, Mere, Newcastle-under-Lyme, then Stone, Rugeley, Litchfield, Stonebridge, Banbury, Oxford, Henley, Maidenhead and Staines – 230 miles

'Thank you' drivers of GYR 882 and LYO 686!

August 1954 – 30 Days Leave

6-25 Sept 1954 – Tour 5 – Wales & SW England

Everyone returned to the depot, much refreshed after such an enjoyable leave, but few felt like any work. However, in true Column style we managed to find ourselves occupied at the harvesting on sports afternoon - as sure a sign as any that we had plenty to do.

And as we sat in the grey murk of the morning of Monday 6th September, little did we think that this tour would be remembered for its hard graft.

This day' ride took us west nor'west to Gloucester, the cathedral city nestling in the hills near the of the mighty River Severn, and en route we passed many interesting places. From Guildford, across the Hog's Back to Farnham and into the land of the Farnborough air show. Then by way of Aldershot, Odiham and Basingstoke to Newbury on the A4 – "The Great West Road". Our run on this fine highway was short-lived, for we branched right at Hungerford for Cricklade and eventually Cirencester. The remaining twenty miles to our night halt at RAF Innsworth were covered at "kangaroo" pace, as at many points we managed to lose sections of the Column in the steep, hilly region of the A417.

RAF Innsworth is a big camp that houses Records Office, 5 PDC and Command Accounts, among other such queer-sounding names. If we found time to take a stroll to the NAAFI, we were soon surrounded by an assortment of RAF "wallas" – all eager to find out how to join the Column and rid themselves of such a place as Innsworth.

Tues September 7th – Innsworth to St Athan

On an exceedingly frosty morning in Gloucestershire we prepared to leave

Innsworth and the conditions account for the low self-starting figures of vehicles this particular day. My Consul was in bad shape all morning, suffering from what sounded like a slipped disc, but what eventually turned out to be oiled-up sparkplugs. Our run was to be a short one, about 90miles, and from the cathedral city we went on the A48 nearly all the way.

Chepstow, the first sizeable place, will always be remembered for its steep hills in the centre of the town, and as soon as we crossed the bridge there, we were in Wales. Traffic was at a standstill as our convoy whined its way up the vertical main street and out of this picturesque town. Engines were given a chance to cool off at the following tea halt and then it was onward to Newport, St Millions and Cardiff, three places which we were to see rather a lot of later in the week.

St Athan is a very small village about ten miles from the fabulous Barry Island and about half a mile from this village is what is said to be the largest RAF camp in Great Britain. We were billeted in the East Camp, which itself is huge compared to many units, and for miles in each direction stretched hangars and RAF buildings. Preparation was in full swing for Battle of Britain displays and

we often had fine views of various types of aircraft practising.

So our first glimpse of this, our base for eight days was quite fair.

Is EMC being run properly? Author challenges militaria. Startling statements against the authorities…

On Weds to Sat the 8th to 11th of September we did four exercises at the following places in South Wales – Cwbran, Bridgend, Cardiff and Newport.

These were all very active affairs and all a considerable distance from base, so by the Saturday, few of us really knew what it felt like to have a good sleep. Matters were not eased by the persistent parades and inspections by our military officers, which seem absolutely unnecessary in the circumstances and grossly against the efficient running of a mobile unit such as ours.

However, despite such treatment by persons obviously unaccustomed and inexperienced in such work, I think the majority of us enjoyed each of the four exercises, some small point always being remembered.

Maintenance continued steadily and at our refuelling point in the village, the pump owner must have made a small fortune from EMC.

Another profitable concern was being new in the form of a caravan snack bar opposite our billets, where everything could be brought including tea at 9d per cup. This concern suitably named "The Barn" did a roaring trade from our fellows, as at that time our own catering arrangements were rather grim.

Eleven hours is quite a time to last on a cup of tea, but believe it or not, that happened on two occasions during the days of the abovementioned exercises. Our views were, of course, suitably voiced when at all possible, but to little avail – Grant and Coy held out!

Meanwhile, the accident rate was fairly low, only a minor ditching being reportable. In this incident, Burgess, one of our MT wonders, managed to drive a CRV into a 12 foot deep entrance for an underground shelter. This brings to mind the parking arrangements when the column left its mark in South Wales by converting a fine acreage of grassland into one of the squelchiest mudbaths on any RAF unit.

And so to Sunday 12th September and the first of two Rest Days on this tour. Spent, amongst other things, in walking along the Bristol Channel coastline from St Athan eastwards to East Aberthaw.

Monday, 13th September – "Soccer"

Heavy rains converted this maintenance day into a semi-rest day, but in the evening, a fair contingent of EMC supporters turned our in oilskins and rubber boots to cheer on their eleven men due to play a St Athan RAF team. Water Polo might have been a better idea for the conditions, but at half time, we were satisfied to see our team holding the "favourites" to a 1-1 draw.

However, the goal-hungry St Athan forwards held their legs longer in the second half and swamped our boys with a further six goals without reply.

Final result:
RAF St Athan East Camp **7** : EMC **1**

PICTURE POST AND EMC

Tues 14th September

After much weeping, wailing and gnashing of gears, the Column found itself on the massive parade ground of St Athan camp and forming up under the directions of two "Picture Post" representatives.

After one and three quarter hours of lining up and shunting to and fro, the photographer took his first shot and others followed, mainly general views of column personnel and vehicles.

Excitement at the though of appearing in Hulton's National Weekly was high and all that was required now was the date of the publication. But more was to come and the photographers accompanied us on Welsh Region Exercise 5 to Swansea. En route they took some shots of the operational column mobile near St Brides Major,[3] in an ideal setting of hills, and apart from that the 45-mile run was uneventful.

A good exercise took place with a welcome meal at its termination, but it was a very tired column which yawned its way back along the coast road via Neath and Port Talbot to Hantivit Major. A CRV with jammed 2nd gear was towed all of 30 miles to base, arriving there at 02.45 hours the following day.

Weds 15th September – Publicity Tour

The first of its kind on Tour 5 and our route, operational column only, was due north via Cowbridge, Hantrisant,

Pontypridd, and Dowlais to Merthyr Tydvil.

On reaching this mining community high in the south welsh hills, the police escort led us on a publicity drive of the town itself, built on a very steep slope, and halted us in a narrow street just off the main thoroughfare.

Then the mayor and his civic accomplices, all sporting the yellow CD armbands, inspected the column, watched by a crowd on inquisitive public and a bevy of beautiful typists from a solicitor's office opposite!

While our officers retired to the Mayor's parlour for you-know-what, we had some minutes to inspect a few of the Tydvil sights, before returning by the same route of 36 miles to base.

Thurs 16th September – St Athan to Norton Fitzwarren

This move marked the end of the Welsh regional section of Tour 5, and much to the annoyance of all TAFFS we were soon re-crossing the border at Chepstow and heading back towards Gloucester.

First piece of activity was in Gloucester, when the Mayor and Civic dignitaries together with our Commandant and

---

[3] Used for the front cover of this book, Ed.

Deputy, took the salute as the column drove past the saluting base in High Street. Next port of call was Stroud, where the local division WVS prepared a midday meal, served in a large marquee just off the main road.

Due south via Chipping Sodbury to Bristol, where the local city police earned themselves a bad reputation by escorting us through in no less than twenty different columns by twenty different routes. The result was that the Column had to reform again on the city boundary and lost considerable time doing this. The escorting was easily the worst we had experienced in all tours so far, so full black marks to Bristol.

By now I had pushed on ahead with the Commandant and CI into Somerset, where, at Bridgwater, eager local CD Corps personnel were all ready to entertain us to tea, in the Drake Halls there.

The column being three quarters of an hour late, however, it did not alter the taste of a very welcome sandwich meal. The mayor had to say a little from the platform and the Brigadier replied for the Column.

Now truly in Somerset, we went 14 miles further south to an army camp near Taunton, at Norton Fitzwarren, where comfortable and welcome accommodation was enjoyed by all.

Friday 17th Sept – Tiverton & Exeter

And off again to our next temporary base, only 48 miles away. In perfect weather, the column wound its way in and out of the dew-covered valleys in Somerset and over the sun-kissed hill into Devon, where our first engagement was the drive past the Mayor or Tiverton.

His Worship appeared from the Guildhall in full dress of fur cloak with red and gold sashes, and walked slowly to the saluting base, an old coal lorry, accompanied by his mace-bearers and henchmen. This was typical of Tiverton, the real old English traditions remaining, and presently the Town Crier appeared with his "Oyez, Oyez" and bell.

A few hours of so-called rest before once more becoming mobile and reaching the golden city of Exeter where we were due to do an exercise. This operation was widely publicised beforehand so there were large contingents of the public at the various incidents. One of the largest of these was at Exercise 'Bridge', where rescue parties had to cross the river by punts before reaching their casualties, while at the British Legion Halls incident, parties had a most realistic bomb-site to tackle.

The Commandant and CO were turfed out of their car and it was used as a sitting case casualty car, so I was guaranteed a more interesting evening conveying sundry cases to hospital.

At the end of the exercise some 400 Column personnel and local divisions were given a sandwich meal in the Civic Halls by the WVS.

Saturday 18 September

A Rest Day and one of the most successful in 1954. It being on a sensible day like a Saturday we could all go out and find shops, etc, open. The majority of us visited Exeter itself and watched the Third Division South game between the local city and Queens Park Rangers. The 2-1 result in favour of the locals was highly cheered by all their fans as they have had a rather lean time this season and the Londoners arrived as favourites. Star of the match was 17-year-old Graham Rees, O/L for Exeter, whom the papers predict as being another Cliff Bastin. St James Park is a fine ground for a 3rd division side, one of the best I have seen.

Sunday 19th September – Plymouth

Had we travelled on the A38 from Exeter we could have reached Plymouth in about 3 hours, but as this highway was "blown up" the Column was diverted on a roundabout network of "B" class roads. Easily one of the hilliest roads and CRV killers we have been on, and at the earliest hour on a Sunday at 7am not everyone felt like tackling these.

While some of "A" Unit slept on the floor of a CRV, a large tea urn containing break for 50 men was overturned on a sharp bend and two fellows were slightly scalded by the steaming cascade of boiling tea. When they managed to attract the attention of their driver, the vehicle was halted and the two unfortunates rushed to hospital at Moreton Hampstead. They were later sent back to base.

Meanwhile, a lot of second gear work was evident as 25 vehicles climbed for three miles, through Moreton Hampstead and onto Dartmoor. When we crossed the sun was out and it was a beautiful morning and all we could see was miles of moorland, riddled with bogs and swamps, stretching for miles. How on earth anyone could get out of such a maze in fog I don't know, but our police escort told us many weird and wonderful tales about escapes from "the Moor."

Our tea break was held in view of Dartmoor Prison, on the outskirts of Princetown, a sight many of us will never forget.

We eventually reached Plymouth and at the RV. The column was deployed to various incidents within this naval port's boundary. One incident was within the barracks of the Royal Marines Commando, so you can assume that extracting the casualties there was quite a proposition.

Lunch was held in a school meals centre in Ocean Street, Swonport and was the biggest washout of Tour 5. Few had a complete lunch and what they had was barely worth the effort of eating! After kit exchange, at Plymouth Argyle FC ground, we returned on the main road to base. Only other happening of note was when D/R "Geordie" Joe Scott upended his cycle in a ditch but suffered no ill, his cycle only receiving a twisted gear lever.

Monday, Sept 20ᵗʰ – Barnstable, Bideford and South Molton

The column left Honiton base in the unusual unit formation of B, C, A and proceeded out of Exeter on the A377. A unit apiece was going to the three Devonshire towns named and "A" Unit were first to drop off when the B3220 was reached. Eight miles later, "C" Unit branched to the right for South Molton with the aid of specially erected AA signs on the roadside.

So "B" Unit continued to Barnstable, on the coastline of Barnstable Bay. On the outskirts of the town, the elderly mayor welcomed us to the ancient burgh and inspected the unit column, before the RV was reached and deployment continued.

On this exercise some most unusual problems were met with, and not the least of these was the rescue of casualties from a main sewer. Two men of "B" Unit rescue parties were sent down and soon found the breathing apparatus more of a hindrance than a help. But they did manage to raise them to the surface, and were very glad to come out of such an unusual place. Owing to a soaking received while underground, the two rescuers were rushed off for a bath and then dispatched back to base by express means.

At Barnstable, a very substantial meal was served by the WVS in a local school, and reports from the other towns say the meal was also a good one. In fact, one of the best exercise meals since Margate in

Tour 1, but not to the standard of Hawick feast.

Base was eventually reached in the earlier hours of Tuesday morning.

Tuesday, Sept 21st – Taunton

On this day, I returned to base in Epsom with the Commandant and had a speedy run through the six English counties of Devon, Somerset, Dorset, Wilts, Hants, and Surrey. Exeter to Camberley, 140miles, was covered in 3 hours 30 minutes.

Meanwhile, the Column was on exercise at Taunton in the land of the cider, and reports state that all went satisfactorily there.

Wed–Fri 22–24 September

The Column spent the first of these days on the move from Honiton to the next temporary base at RAF Compton Bassett. The route was due northeast, via Yeovil, Wincanton and Frome to the camp, which is near Calne in Wiltshire.

The following day, Thursday, was the exercise at Swindon, a shore run of 16 miles away, and on Friday, the operational column returned to Bristol – the scene of one of the Column's most chaotic escorts

to date. On this visit, things were not much better, and although the exercise went off quite well, the policing did not. Once again, there were groups of two and threes CRVs and an odd Austin shooting all over the city, lost from the rest, and the resulting shambles took quite a bit of sorting out.

Sat Sept 25th – Back to Epsom

Much rejoicing in the camp at the prospect of returning to Epsom and its attachments and no one was sorry to leave the RAF camp at 08.00 hours and proceed on the most direct route of Marlborough, Newbury, Basingstoke, Odiham, Aldershot, Guildford-by-pass, Leatherhead by-pass and Epsom.

First to arrive in base was the MT towing the winch vehicle, but the had left Calne at 5 a.m. and they were followed by several small advance parties, the main column arriving about 1.30 p.m. Then followed a mad rush to have lunch, collect passes and proceed on four days unofficial leave, the result of ingenious thought by our CO, combining September and October 48-hour passes.

108 miles.

So ended Tour 5 in the lands of coal, cider, clotted cream and sausages.

Tuesday 5th October – Publicity Drive – Surrey

This drive lasted for over four hours plus a lunch halt at Mitcham. The operational column covered nearly all of Surrey and much of the tour was in heavy traffic, in the Mitcham, Streatham and Wimbledon areas, but some pleasant countryside was traversed in the districts of Coulsdon, Purley and Banstead.

At Kingston, the column was inspected by the Lord Lieutenant of the County, General Sir Robert Haining and the Chairman of the County Council, Sir John Wenham. Following this, refreshments were provided. Lunch was taken at the Canons Mitcham.

The following County boroughs were covered, Esher, Surbiton, Kingston, Richmond, Barnes, Malden, Coombe, Wimbledon, Merton, Morden, Mitcham, Sutton, Cheam, Carshalton, Beddington, Wallington, Coulsdon, Purley, Banstead and Epsom – 20.

Fri 8th October 1954 – Tour 6 – North East England and North Midlands

It began a quiet, damp and misty morning, but this atmosphere was soon altered when the column moved off on Tour 6. The first halt, luckily for only one night was at the dreaded Rufford Abbey, near Ollerton. Again, more than two thirds of the troops slept in the vehicles and we were all glad to know that that was to be out last visit there.

The following day, Sat. 9th October, a journey of only 60 miles was needed before the column reached its temporary base of the N.E. region, at Sherburn-in-Elmet, Yorkshire. Here we were billeted in a disused Ministry of Works hostel in the centre of a housing estate in this small and sleepy Yorkshire village.

Sunday, 10th October 1954 – Bradford

A large-scale exercise took place in Bradford involving our sector control, which set off as usual several hours before the main operational column. Not much information has been collected about this exercise, the first in Yorkshire (N.E. region).

Monday, 11th October 1954

On this maintenance day for the column at Sherburn, I travelled north with the Commandant from Epsom via Camberley. The round trip of 239 miles, was covered in good weather at an average speed of 30-40mph and was quite uneventful. The route from

Camberley was on the A30 to Chiswick roundabout, then the North Circular Rd, round to the A1, which we held all the way to Brotherton, then A162 – Sherburn.

Tuesday 12th October – Dewsbury

This was the first evening exercise of five in five days, and only two units took part, these being "A" and "B" units. En route, which was via Garforth, Swillington and Tingley, all of Baker unit plus some of Andrew became detached and the column was held up for quite a time. However, after losing all four D/Rs we reached RV on time and reunited with out wandering comrades.

The exercise took place in the surface buildings of a local coalmine and everything was really quite normal. All operations were done by floodlight, a new feature on all exercises on the tours from now on. Light refreshments of soup, tea and biscuits were enjoyed by all in a barn near the mine, following which the column left on return to base.

Wednesday 13th October – Floodlit Parade, York

This turned out to be one of the biggest gatherings of CD personnel that EMC

has taken part in this year. The column of two units, A and C arrived in good time in the centre of York, and under police guidance, formed up in the wide Parliament Street. We were followed by CD contingents from all around and soon the long street was a seething mass of CRVs, ambulances, AFS tenders, Food Flying Squad vans and every possible kind of Civil Defence people.

While music was supplied by the Leeds City Police Band, our inspection party of fifteen, inspected all the assembled services. It was headed by the recently appointed Director General of Civil Defence, Sir Sydney Kirknans, and included the Lord Mayor or York, an Assistant Under Secretary of State, Yorkshire CDO and Brigadier McKenzie.

Following this gruelling half hour stand to attention, the FFS supplied a wonderful hot cup of tea and 1,100 paper bags of sausage rolls, sandwiches and cake were distributed by the WVS. A dance followed.

Thursday 14th October – Exercise "Lucifer" – Barnsley

This exercise, involving mobile sector control and only one unit, B, of EMC was a great washout.

In heavy rain the Column left base at 1700 hours and proceeded due south east via Wakefield, until the RV was reached, a few miles out of Barnsley. Owing to heavy road traffic the police guides were not happy with the smallish column at the RV, so we moved in for another mile, and patiently awaited instructions from main control.

These took a long time in coming, and during our wait of 55 minutes we lost six road sentries by drowning in the torrential downpour.

All through the exercise, it rained, but not just rain, soot as well, and everyone was thoroughly fed up after a few hours of such conditions. The incidents were mainly in an old glasshouse area, off the main Barnsley-Pontefract road and work was covered by our own limited floodlighting apparatus, when it was noted that the limited lights we have are not adequate for a complete exercise.

In a brewery canteen, tea and ham sandwiches were served to those who had survived, and our column returned in the early hours of Friday morning, "fair drookit."

Friday 15th October – Exercise "Flashlight" – ICI – Huddersfield

An early start was called for, so tea was served in picnic fashion by the side of the Leeds-Huddersfiled A62. All operations took place within the works of ICI and as we entered, all matches, cigarettes etc, were confiscated. A rather unusual exercise in that each incident had its own particular hazards depending on which plant it happened to be in. Rubber boots had to be worn by all rescue parties, and in some cases, special type respirators were issued.

All around this huge chemical works, tanks of coloured liquids and gases aroused great suspicion and it was undoubtedly an amazing experience. Two parties dealt with casualties trapped under railway carriages in a works siding, but most were dealing with incidents peculiar to rescue such a factory.

When rescue operations ceased, by the sounding of fire sirens, the operational column received an interesting lecture from one of the ICI Civil Defence Chiefs. In fact several of us voted him as our best lecturer yet, because good is the man who can hold his audience, with a subject like that, after several hours of rescue have been done.

Following this, we visited the very modern works canteen for a supper of tea, coffee, pies, sandwiches and cakes. We ate all we possibly could and still there was more, so pockets and haversacks were filled with the delicacies. An excellent meal. It was very welcome, taking into account the fact that our meals at base have been below standard so far.

In both ICI factories we have visited – Billingham (Tour 4) and Huddersfield (Tour 6) – the canteen and meals have been of an exceptionally high standard, and far above a normal WVS post-exercise meal.

Saturday, 16th October – York

Not much of an exercise, involving three units of EMC, one for deployment purposes only. Bad weather made this a wasted Saturday afternoon, and bad timing organization made all column personnel fed up. One wait of 50 minutes six miles from York was fantastic, and two hours after the RV report, some parties were still waiting for deployment. In fact, the only charming factor in a very miserable Saturday, was a hot knife and fork meal served by WVS in Fulford Road School.

For Scots, of course, a cheering bit of news was the international result from Cardiff (Wales 0 Scotland 1).

Sunday 17-10-54 – Maintenance Day

Monday 18-10-54 – Rest Day

Tuesday 19th October 1954

Operational Column move Sherburn to Proteus camp via Sheffield (inspection) Admin Column move Sherburn –Proteus (direct).

This was a long and tiring day for all who travelled with the Operational Column. Leaving Sherburn hostel at 1000hrs, the Column made good speed through Doncaster, Rotherham, to a few miles outside the Sheffield city boundary, where our kitchens were set up. As we were ahead of time, a long wait was made and this started a heavy day of nothing but killing time. When we eventually reached the city centre, the Lord Mayor inspected all personnel and some of the vehicles parked on the street outside the City Hall. This event lasted for approx half an hour before we were on the road again and due south to Chesterfield, 12 miles away. Again parking in the town square, we had a few minutes to look around the shops before the Flying

Squad (North Midlands Convoy) served us with tea. We met these ladies on our travels before and their food was of the usual high standard. Then south again and via Edwinstowe, Bolsover and the Sherwood Forest, we arrived at No. 12 WETC, Proteus, near Ollerton at 18.00 hours.

Meantime, the Admin Column had left Yorkshre at 1100hrs and arrived at base three hours later. For all the good we did at S and C we may as well have come straight South too.

Wednesday 20th October, 1954 – Exercise "Lindum" – Lincoln

The best part of the day was spent settling in to this concentration camp, in the middle of the Forest. Miles from the nearest village, Ollerton, it lies half a mile from the main A614. It is made up of a collection of dilapidated Nissen Huts, which neither keep out the wind or rain, nor let in any warmth, and has been voted easily the worst camp we have ever stayed at.

The exercise was a good one, because it got off to a good start, with tea in a school meals centre in LinColumn The Mayor dressed in full evening dress, looked in while we were eating and gave us a short, interesting, and very amusing speech. He was en route to a dinner with the Licensed Victuallers Association. The meal, like all exercise meals on this North Midlands section of this tour, was excelled.

No outstanding problems were evident at the various incidents and all went off well. It was evident that quite a deal of publicity had been made of the exercises, as the public were out in force at each incident. The Sector Control on exhibition spent the evening with Joyce and Jean, two nice local girls not partial to coffee.

Thurs 21st & Sat 23rd Oct 1954

These days were spent journeying to and from two East Coast RAF stations, Manby and North Coates. The Column was forced to stay there to enable them to do an exercise in Grimsby, and as neither station could not take the whole Column, it had to be split - "B" Unit to Manby, and "A" and "C" Units to North Coates. Reports state that Manby was a good camp with excellent food, while North Coates, like our base, was miles from anywhere and had poor food and quarters.

Lincolnshire is a county riddled with service establishments and the countryside was most uninteresting –

miles and miles of flat land and hardly a tree to be seen, but good road surfaces with bad bends.

On the other hand, Nottingham County can take full marks for roads. They are excellent width and good surface, and I doubt if there is another county in England to compare.

The day between the two journeys was Friday 22nd and the day of the exercise. I travelled direct to Grimsby via Lincoln and Louth, and arrived at the RV for Baker unit in New Waltham, in food time to tag on with that unit and proceed to the incident. This was in the British Electricity Authority Power Station, and for quite a while, the activities there seemed most unlike a CD exercise, for not an ambulance or local person was to be seen.

Meanwhile, "A" and "C" Units were making their way into the city centre to the CD HQ – a converted church building. There an enjoyable meal of Shepherds Pie and Potatoes, sandwich, butter roll, slab cake, and tea plus an apple, was available to all. These units then did their exercise, while B, having completed their tasks, made for tea.

The second half of CD operations took place mainly in the docks, where there were some interesting problems. The rescue parties should by now be well acquainted with the various smells attached to some rescue operations – Grimsby Docks were no exception!

Continuing in the usual EMC style, we spent Saturday afternoon in this desolate hotel, imagining how our respective soccer teams were fairing. And *imagine* was all we could do.

Sun 24th October 1954 – Billesden – Hinckley – Loughborough

At the unearthly Sunday morning hour of 5.30am we were rudely awakened to prepare to move on Exercise "L". At 7am the Operational Column, plus our Mobile Sector Control, moved from between the dead oaks of Robin Hood Land and wheezed its way in a southerly direction on the A614/A46 to Leicester.

Soon after crossing the county border and some miles north of the city, we had tea and biscuits from a small mobile WVS van, but the atrocious weather conditions prevented this snack being enjoyed in comfort. Heavy rains continued all morning and some parts of the roads had to be traversed cautiously, owing to deep "dubs" forming. From the RV, A, B and C Units were deployed to the towns of Loughborough, Hinckley, and Billesden respectively, all being some 10 miles out of Leicester city and a good 25 miles apart. From all reports the problems of rescue were quite satisfactory and provided no obstacle to our highly efficient squadron.

Besides getting well soaked, lunch was provided by Local Authority in each town. The Loughborough contingent get top marks for serving a glorious meal in the works canteen of Henry Morris (Cranes). Other units were not so fortunate.

Monday 25-10-54 – Rest Day

A Rest Day to EMC at Proteus is about as much good as Glasgow Fair Holiday is to the Antarctic Explorers. However, for once the rains stopped and several persons got out into civilization. Namely, those who went on an organised trip round the works of Ruston and Horsnby, Lincoln, and those who took advantage of bus runs to Mansfield and Nottingham.

Tues October 26 – Nottingham

Following the usual EMC pattern, we had an energetic morning on maintenance and in the evening exercise in Nottingham.

Bad weather marred the exercise in this attractive city and not much was to be seen through the driving rain. These conditions could not, however, explain the loss of Mr Bone and "C"U – the former eventually pulling into a side of the road and crying his little heart out for help. Not that that was our first experience of such behaviour. The D/Rs flatly and rightly refused to look for him as they have long bemoaned his inability to close up, but his eventual rescue must be attributed to the efficient and alert A/C Down, R, in charge of mobile sector control.

Not being acquainted with the rigours of rescue, I make no comment of the problems experienced by this section.

An excellent meal of steak & kidney pie and peaches, cream and cherry jelly gateau was had by all in a school meal centre. Top Marks!

Wednesday, October 27 – Leicester

Leicester being about 45 miles away we had an early start in the afternoon and on the A614-A6079 and A46 reached the outskirts of this first division football city. The police guides then discovered we had come too far, so it was 'about-turn' in the dual carriageway and along a narrow lane we went round the city and arrived at the modern secondary school for tea. Another good one.

No comments on the following exercise.

Thurs October 28th – Proteus to Stoneleigh Park Camp, Coventry

The second last move of Tour 6 and no one was sorry, for by now each and everyone was becoming more than browned off. For publicity reasons, the route was much longer than necessary and the whole convoy moved through the rolling countryside of Notts, Leics and Northants into Warwickshire via Oakham, Uppingham and Market Harborough, before lunch in a small village lay-by and the remaining run through Rugby to Stoneleigh (A445).

The camp, another weekend training camp, but slightly more alive than the dead Proteus, is about four miles from "CD banned" Coventry. But accommodation was again very poor and much objection was made to the state of our quarters when we moved in. I suspect the Column is often being used to give such places their annual spring-clean, and it really is not good enough. The main idea then was to bed down in preparation for the very long day ahead.

Friday 29th October 1954

At 14.00 hours the operational column left en route for Epsom via a Northampton exercise, and next to leave was the Admin Column, en route for Epsom direct.

From reports received, the latter's run south was rather slow and uneventful except when Column Commander Mr Ashdown nearly had his lot at the hand of LYO 727, driven by A/C Fitch and aided by Gunner Petrie (both "Jocks"). The Admin Column reached Epsom at 23.15 hours.

Meanwhile, the WVS gave "operational plus sector control" a sandwich tea in a disused stable shed near Northampton, and then we set off for the RV via a 20-mile country lane diversion, which caused the Brigadier to review the petrol situation for the notice of his superiors.

Eventually, the rescue parties were deployed, s/c set up, and a very excellent exercise took place.

At a meal by WVS in the city fire station followed, and we had good speeches from His Worship the Mayor, the Column Commandant, and Mr Briggs the Regional Officer.

The Brigadier paid a great compliment to the people of Northampton and district who undoubtedly had organised a very tidy exercise, involving much preparation beforehand and thinking. Recruiting figures for Northampton are very high and one has reason to believe it possesses some excellent rescue and operational parties. In contrast, the weak stew, hard potatoes and poor tea was most disappointing.

At 10 p.m. we left the fire station HQ and said "goodbye" to Northampton as we headed towards the A5, which we reached at Towcester. Then it was a steady 25mph on this highway, busy with a fair amount of heavy traffic. Apart from a few halts for natural reasons, the only other halt was in the "Old Road" north of Dunstable, where a FDV under the expert cooking of Mr "Philbert" Thorne gave us hot dogs and rolls with tea.

After a run via St. Albans the North Circular Rd, Chiswick Roundabout and Kew Bridge, we reached the camp again at a few minutes after 3 a.m.

Bed for a couple of hours, more unnecessary maintenance and then we had three days stand-down, long overdue. The overnight run from Northampton was a great success, but Tour 6 was voted as being rather poor – bad organisation

being the hallmark and some poor accommodation.

No further comments on this, the second longest tour of EMC 1954.

Tour 7 – 11-21 November 1954 – Southern England

The original itinerary for this tour told us we were to have a base at RAF Booker, but after a recce of this station when conditions were found to be unsuitable, our sojourn there was cancelled and activities conducted from Epsom.

The first of these, on Thursday 11th November 1954 was exercise in Aldershot, the home of the British Army. The column rendezvoused on the Guildford/Aldershot Road near the Blue Parrot and from there were deployed to Aldershot and district. One incident with two parties at work was inside the secret Royal Aircraft Establishment at Farnborough, and during this usual tour of operations, the Commandant could not convince the gate-hands that he had anything to do with the exercise, and was refused admission. Two parties went to the Rushmere Arena, where casualties were trapped in the huge grandstands. It was a sorry sight to see such a wonderful natural arena going to waste, but there were obvious signs of this, and I hear only a yearly horse show is held in this Aldershot 'Wembley'.

A meal of tea, sausage roll, sandwiches and slab cake was served from one of our Food Distribution Vans in the Blue Parrot car park before the operational column returned about 11.30p.m.

Fri 12ᵗʰ Nov– Rest and Maintenance

Saturday, 13ᵗʰ Nov – Reading

Only "B" and "C" Units were out this exercise. Leaving camp at 11am, the smaller column, in command of Major J.W. Nicolson, proceeded via Hampton Court Bridge and Staines to Ascot.

There "Jock" Grant and a staff of three gave us for a lunch one of the weakest stews in column history, most of which found its way to the nearest drain. So, it was in an aggressive mood that the Column continued via the A329 Virginia Water – Reading – Wokingham road to RV at the "Green Monkey."

The main incident was in the large biscuit factory of Huntley & Palmer Ltd, while smaller incidents were at corporation yards and blitzed houses. Tea was had in Newtown School, Liverpool Street, and the return run over the same

route was made between 1730 and 1930hrs.

Sunday, 14ᵗʰ Nov – Slough & Oxford

"A" and "C" Units went to Slough at 9am and returned at 15.00 hours, but "B" Unit, on the longer run, left Epsom at 1000hrs and had lunch just north of Henley-on-Thames. This was provided by tireless "Philbert" Thorne and his FDV and this wonderful worker travelled with us all day, providing several snacks and welcome cups of tea.

The unit was fairly well spread out over the university city, and I spent most of the time at sector control, where members of Oxford Vespa Club acted as guides and messengers. A snack was provided by emergency feeding WVS in a gaily painted nissen hut known as *Crowsham Marsh Restaurant*.

The run back was made in total darkness and took about 2½ hours.

Tuesday 16ᵗʰ Nov – RAF Titchfield

Yours truly did not travel with the column on this particular run when they left base at 10.00 hours under Metropolitan Police escort. The route was on the A246 Leatherhead bypass, Guildford bypass, Farnham, Alton and the Winchester bypass A33 to Fareham. Lunch was on the last named bypass and at the stage "C" Unit parted company with the main column and headed for Chickerell Camp, near Weymouth, from where they were due to attend the Weymouth exercise.

At RAF Titchfield the remainder settled down in fairly good quarters to await further developments. The only excitement in an otherwise uneventful day was when the prize dunderhead Stubley "pranged" his POV into the last CRV Bakery Unit. The unfortunate vehicle, GLT 677, was later towed to base by an MT vehicle with heavy denting on the nearside, especially the wing, which all by disappeared into the engine casing.

Owing to lack of material, reports on the following day's events are withheld:

Weds 17th – Friday 19th November

The main events were concerning "C" Unit at Weymouth on the Wednesday, and "A" unit on Exercise "Cutlass" at Bournemouth.

Friday forenoon was a publicity drive of the Operational Column and certain admin vehicles through Portsmouth and district, while in the evening, we had Exercise "Discovery II" in the naval capital itself. Firstly, our officers had to attend the usual dinner and wines from government funds in the Nuffield Centre, – it would not do for these gentlemen not to justify their £1,500 per year!

Main control was a Fort Widley – a bomb disposal unit camp high on the hills overlooking the coast – formerly a fort in the Napoleonic Wars.

Saturday, 20th Nov – Southampton

The local authorities in this manoeuvre seemed extremely keen to have a whale of a day and from all reports Southampton was said to have had a severe taste of enemy aggression. The exercise name was "Survival."

The Column after leaving camp at 1pm arrived at the RV at 2pm on the Fareham-East High Road, and there were met by police guides, who took each unit to their respective Post Controllers for deployment.

All the usual services were present with walkie-talkie girls all round the city, and ambulances bearing "L" plates grinding to and fro.

Sector control as usual was comfortably settled down on Pear Tree Green where Messrs Down, Phipson and Christmas amused themselves by cooking their own meals. Our two Irish control operators, John "Paddy" Christmas and Ray "Dullie" Little were particularly prominent.

Tea was enjoyed by some in a realistic building partly demolished, given by the WVS, and an after-exercise conference was held in the majestic Civic Centre.

Sunday, 21st Nov – back to Epsom

General feeling was that we could easily have done the return run of 65 miles after the exercise the night before, but you know what our shower are, so at 8.30am off we went and on the same route as Tuesday, only in reverse, came back to jolly old Epsom more or less in one piece at 12 noon.

Apart from it being a Sunday, the time was then ripe to return on the 3-day stand-down but, 'oh no, that would never do,' says Mr Dobbing, sipping coffee and reading *The People*. 'Certainly not,' says Ignoramus Bone, bawling his bloomin' 'ead orf at Jock Macgregor, who merely suggested breaking that officer's neck with an axe! So at 4pm the boys eventually made out of the camp on the stand-down, while Messrs Bone and Dobbing retired among their worn cobwebs. Here I end Tour Seven.

Yours Truly, Disgusted.

Tour 8 – 2-12 Dec 1954 – London Region

By now, very well browned off with Column exercises, it was with mixed feelings that we started the eighth and last tour of EMC 1954. Almost our shortest tour, it was made up of seven exercises in total, five deployment and two rescue.

Thurs 2nd Dec – Lambeth & Wandsworth

A deployment exercise, this one turned out to be easily the column's worst organised exercise from an operational point of view. The Sector Control, situated in Brockwell Park Gardens, was the complete example of chaotic disorganisation, and each and every one of our efficient operators, cast out into the street, loudly bemoaned such actions.

Saturday, 4th Dec – Woolwich

Another deployment-only manoeuvre, this was of a much higher standard operationally, despite the fact that the local forces were late in arrival at the RV, the result being tea in Sid's Café for all.

The eighteen rescue vehicles were sent all over the burgh of Woolwich to various warden posts and near the end, tea was being served at the CD HQ.

Verdict – Fair to good.

Sunday 5th Dec – Middlesex

The first rescue exercise of the tour, and an early start from the depot to reach the RV on the North Circular Road at the Abbey Hotel.

Various incidents in the areas of Harlesden, Willesden, Wembley and Cricklewood, with a fair meal in a Willesden school at 13.00 hours.

No further comment.

Tuesday, 7th Dec – City of London

Quite a busy evening, which included a display by two CRVs and crews at St Swithin's House, home of the Shell-Mex BP factory. Meanwhile the column had arrived in Holborn and were deployed in Finsbury area, while the Commandant lost himself in Central London en route to Finsbury Town Hall. His subsequent lament on the R/T helped to keep the party going, and this all ended at 9.30pm with tea and sandwiches at CD HQ.

Also an eventful evening for Sector Control with "Fangio" in 684 collecting a puncture and Jim Paul making a real hash of a "Rover 14" in the Strand.

Wednesday 8th Dec – Lambeth / Wandsworth

On paper, this looked to be a repeat of the first exercise, but we did manage to find new parts of these London suburbs, to operate in. Certainly the rescue vehicle drivers had one of their greatest driving experiences in course of deployment. It was an amazing sight to see CRVs coming and going in all directions, or halted at four sides of a junction, overtaking and meeting sister wagons, for a solid 90 minutes. From Lambeth Town Hall, the column eventually gathered and wound a weary homeward run to Epsom.

Saturday, 11th Dec – Essex – Barking

The column caused much chaos in the thick of London's rush traffic as its way wound via London Bridge and East India Dock Road, over the border into the county of Essex.

At Dagenham Docks, the rescue parties embarked on tow RMVR landing craft and were conveyed upstream and landed on a beachhead at Creekmouth. From there, they march over marshes to a BEA power station, where several incidents had been arranged.

A good exercise from the rescue side, but two units had deployment only and were somewhat uselessly employed. A welcome soup tea from WVS in Mission Hall Lane, and in threatening fog. The column returned to base via London Bridge and Clapham Common.

Sun 12th Dec – Kent –Orpington

This was the last exercise of the Column in 1954 and quite a memorable one it turned out to be. The route to Orpington was, as far as it went, the exact same as that we took on the first column move of Tour 1 (May 5), that is, via Reigate, Redhill, Brasted and Westerham. All deployment went on in the areas around Bromley and Orpington and at the close the Chairman of the county council made a speech by the roadside on the use we had been throughout the year.

The return was much quicker, and was via Croydon and Cheam.

And so ended the last Column run of the year, and this heralds' the end of my little report, but before I close, I must report on…

Demonstrations to VIPs – 3rd & 10th December 1954

Before the column finally disbanded on 31st December 1954 we had to put on two rescue demonstrations to parties of VIPs who visited the depot.

The first of these was made up of high ranking officers from the three services, the War Office, the Admiralty and the Air Ministry. About 30 of these arrived in various types of car – from a Group Captain's chauffeur-driven Humber to a Wing Commander in a rusty old Hillman.

A most realistic demonstration of rescue work in relation to the Mobile Column was carried out in the short time available and in conclusion the officers were entertained by our mess to tea.

This visit would no doubt play a great part in the future of Civil Defence and the Armed Forces.

The second visit, one week later, included no less than three Cabinet Ministers. They were the Home Secretary, Mr Gwilym Lloyd George, The Secretary of State for War, Mr Anthony Head, and The Minister of Defence, Harold McMillan.

They were accompanied by small contingents of their followers and a repeat of last week's show was most successfully carried out.

The press and BBC, plus representatives from Gaumont Newsreels were also present and an account of the demonstration was given in that evening's *Radio Newsreel*.

Photo 8. Jim Carson, with Ford Consul staff car.

Photo 9 (a) and (b) EMC Rescue Unit 'A'

3 Reg Barnes	18 Paddy Callaghan	33 ?	48 Sgt. McGuinness
4 Geoff Pogson	19 Dave Wait	34 ?	49 A T Sandy Brown
5 Robin G. Reid	20 ?	35 ?	50 Cap Farol
6 Benn	21 ?	36 ?	51 FO John Birch
7 John Shepperd	22 ?	37 Colgon	52 ?
8 ?	23 George Shore	38 ?	53 John Hudson
9 ?	24 ?	39 Cyril Griffin	54 Tony New
10 Bernard Nice	25 Derek Muggleton	40 ?	55 ?
11 ?	26 Cyril Lester	41 ?	56 ?
12 ?	27 Les Jeffries	42 ?	57 ?
13 Danny Brecknock	28 O'Brien	43 Mackley	58 Barber
14 Ernie Barnes	29 Fred Pleece	44 John Austin	59 Colin Flexman
15 Ray Wilson	30 ?	45 ?	
16 ?	31 Doug Martin	46 Johnson	
17 Gerry Peake	32 Harold Matson	47 Mr Triptree	

Photo 10 (a) and (b) EMC Rescue Unit 'B'

1	Norman Cole	14	Ernie Barnes	41	FO John Birch
2	Derek Hutchinson	16	Peter Hollingsworth	46	Derek Dandridge
3	Brian Steven	18	Hamish Rutherford	47	Terry Adams
6	George Hall	19	Clive Brunton	48	Ron Albiston
7	Malcolm Bidder	20	Derek Holland	51	Ivan Nichols
8	Ralf Baker	22	Des Wilson	52	Reg Haines
9	Peter Cox	36	Scrubber Jones	53	Colin Mason
12	Tom Rigby	39	Sgt Harry Stubley	54	Ken Fiddler
13	Phil Carlington	40	Major Nicholson	45	Joe Windsor

Photo 11 (a) and (b) EMC Rescue Unit 'C'

1. A C Rose, 618	14. A/C Carter, 873	27. A/C Symes, 682	39. Gnr. Powell, 175
2. A/C Lambert, 063	15. A/C Lynch, 201	28. Gnr. Thurlow, 171	40. Mr. Hadden
3. Gnr. Wilson, 490	16. A/C Davison, 557	29. A/C Leydon, 877	41. FO John Bone
4. A/C Taylor, 875	17. A/C Crooks, 158	30. A/C MacGregor, 072	42. Mr Wills
5. Gnr. Foster, 450	18. A/C Hughes, 003	31. A/C Richards-	43. Sgt Lawson
6. A/C Scott, 058	19. A/C Thrower, 146	Davies, 418	44. Mr Ashdown
7. A/C Corran, 968	20. A/C Hippey, 499	32. Gnr. Bensley, 857	45. A/C Mockford, 677
8. A/C Tylor, 478	21. A/C Cable, 474	33. Gnr. Lewis, 006	46. A/C Pearson, 849
9. A/C Sadler, 147	22. A/C Mason, 682	34. A/C Atkins, 507	47. Gnr Patrie, 930
10. Gnr. McAllan, 135	23. A/C Quealy, 808	35. A/C Pescador, 059	48. Gnr Sherwood, 590
11. Gnr. Hodgkins, 008	24. A/C McGugan, 470	36. A/C Costello, 859	49. Gnr Cummings 897
12. A/C Lindley, 860	25. Gnr. Walter	37. Gnr. Marwood, 865	50. A/C Brear, 567
13. A/C Spradbury, 774	26. Gnr. Walters, 26?	38. A/C Payne, 369	

Photo 12. 'D' Group
Gray – Wrathall – Embling – Holms – Birch – Carson – Paull – Down – Phipson – Mitchell
Wright (on m/c) – Cooper – Wiltshire – Christmas – Little – White (on m/c)
Chivers – Price – Lieutenant Patton – Mr Booker – Mr Cox – Mr Triptree

Photo 13. A Rescue team with their vehicle.

Photo 14. HQ Staff – both Service and Civil Defence. (from left)
W/O Stubbs, Major Benny, Mr Wills, Mr Evans, Brigadier McKenzie, Captain Oxbury,
Lieutenant Brown, Squadron Leader Dobbin, Flight Lieutenant Bone, Major Higham,
Major Nicholson, Flight Lieutenant Birch.

Photo 15. Comms Section.
Johnnie Christmas – Frank Wrathall – John Bacon – Mr A.E. Booker – Ray Wiltshire – Ray Down – Ray Little
Don Phipson – J. Paull – Jim Carson – J. Mitchell

Photo 16. Kiln Lane, Epson training ground.

Photo 17. Spreadeagle Hotel at night.

**Photo 18. Lifting gear in use –
Kiln Lane training ground.**

**Photo 19. Lowering a stretcher from a roof
Kiln Lane training ground.**

Photo 20. The Epsom Depot at Kiln Lane.

Photo 21. Lowering a stretcher in a tricky rescue situation.

Photo 22. Mr Triptree, instructor.

Photo 23. Norman Whitaker and Alf Hart in a recovery vehicle.

Photo 24. Rescue team members (l to r) Colin Flexman, Cyril Griffin & Gerry Peake.

Photo 25. Taking the air on the cliffs at Beachy Head.

Photo 26. Some of those wonderful WVS ladies.

Photo 27. Cyril Lester and Gerry Peake out on an exercise.

Photo 28. Snaking hosepipes in a dockland exercise.

Photo 29. Comms Store Van with generator for battery charging. Field cable laying Land Rover in background. Dave Walter, Jay and Jim Watkins.

Photo 30. Captain Farol (instructor) and Sgt McGuiness.

Photo 31. Chief Instructor Captain Oxbury.

Photo 32. Recovery vehicle and team.

Photo 33. Fred Holmes, Brian Birch, Sgt 'Bomber' Price, Steven 'Lefty' Wright, Charlie Cooper.

Photo 34. Bernard Nice at the wheel of a personnel carrier, Seaforth Barracks 1954..

Photo 35. Robin G. Reid, Seaforth Barracks 1954.

Photo 36. WRVS ladies – Worthing.

Photo 37. Cpt Farol, F/Lt John Bone, Brigadier McKenzie, F/Lt John Birch, Lt Sandy Brown.

Photo 38. Donald Millar, Cyril Lester, Sgt McGuiness, Bernard Nice, John Sheppard, Gerry Peake.

Photo 39. Lt Sandy Brown, Sqn Ldr Dobbin ("the Old Grey Mare"), F/Lt John Bone.

Photo 40. Mr Coulson (driving instructor from Chiswick), Bernard Nice, Robin G. Reid.

Photo 41. Unidentified instructor, Mr Triptree (instructor).

Photo 42. Rescue team on and exercise, location unknown.

Photo 43. Cpl Dave Chivers and Ray Down with the HQ Section Radio van.

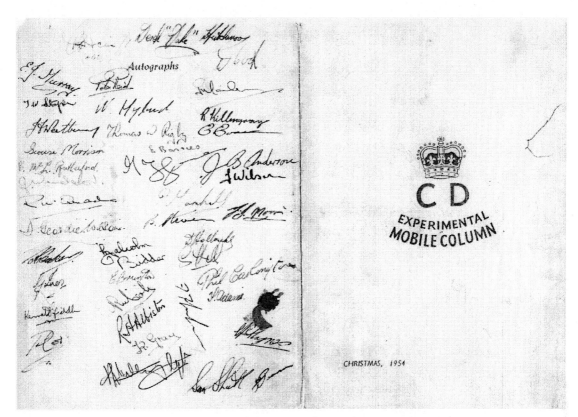

Photo 44. EMC Christmas Card 1954 plus signatures.

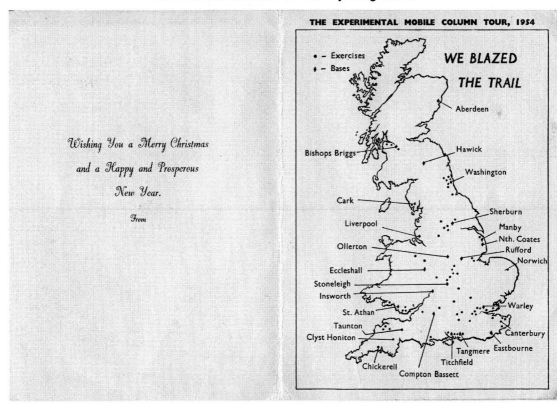

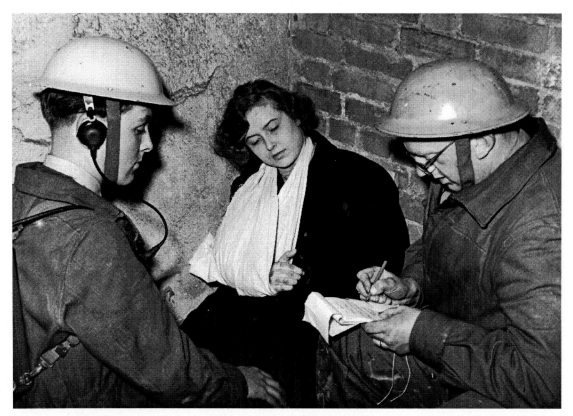

Photo 45. David Chivers on the radio while Sergeant Worth takes details from an attractive young 'victim' on an exercise at Southampton.

Photo 46. Radio van in use at the Coventry demonstration.

Photo 47. Signals Section on Epsom Downs.

Photo 48. Column enters Aberdeen.

Photo 49. The Column on parade for the Picture Post.

Photo 50. Epsom Camp football team.

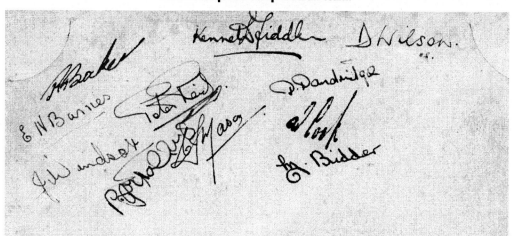

Photo 51 Signatures of the team.

Photo 52. CRV in a spot of bother.

Photo 53. Rescue Team with ladders at the ready plus the full kit they carried.

Photo 54. The Brigadier greeted by yet another Mayor.
F/Lt John Birch, Brg McKenzie, Curly White, Mayor, Maj Nicholson, ???, Sgt Harry Stubley.

Photo 55. The EMC field kitchen, somewhere in England.

Photo 56. NAAFI break – Sgt Lawson, F/Lt John Birch and Brian Birch enjoy 'tea and a wad' from the WRVS Food Flying Squad – their pale blue vans were always a welcome sight.

Photo 57. Sergeant Stubley, A/C McQuade, A/C Bunton and Gnr Cook are shown the benefits of a 'dustbin oven'.

Photo 58. The NAAFI Wagon.

Photo 59. Taffy Evans in the NAAFI Wagon.

Photo 60. EMC Rescue Units demonstrate their skills to a crowd of onlookers on an exercise in badly damaged Cotton Mill in Rochdale.

Photo 61. Robin G. Reid at London Transport Depot, Chiswick with LYR 473.

Photo 62. The very same vehicle, still going strong in Kent over 50 years later.

Photo 63. standing, from left: David Chivers, ??, Les Reid, John Sheppard, John Westbury, Bernard Nice, Bomber Price, Mr Tony Hadden, Sergeant Pullen, Harold Matson, Reg Hains, ??, Robin G. Reid, Scully. Squatting Jones, Derek Dandridge, ??.

Photo 64. DJ Martin, Gerry Barnes, John Hudson, Jerry Peake, R Wilson and WF Childs.

Photo 65. EMC Motorcycle Dispatch Riders.

Photo 66. DRs Holmes, Grey, Compton and Hill on Horseguards Parade.

Photo 67. Tour 7 – Portsmouth – 19 November 1954 – EMC Dispatch Riders.

Photo 68 (a) Despatch rider Geordie Joe Scott performs a dangerous manoeuvre.

Photo 69. Edward Murray and Terry Ransom.

Photo 70. Ivan Nichols, Harry Stubley, Derek Dandridge, Derek Holland, Peter Hollingsworth, Malcolm Bidder.

Photo 71. 50th anniversary cake at our reunion.

Photo 72. Robin G. Reid, Jonathan Reed Mayor of Epsom, Wing Cdr John Birch.

Former EMC Personnel (traced) 2008

1. Albiston, Ron
2. Anderson, Brian
3. Atkins, Brian
4. Baker, Ralph
5. Barnes, Ernie
6. Barnes, Reg
7. Bidder, Malcolm
8. Birch, Brian
9. Birch, John
10. Blackburn, Eric
11. Bone, John
12. Brown, Alex
13. Cable, Gerald
14. Cambridge, Bernard
15. Carson, Jim
16. Childs, Bill
17. Chivers, David
18. Christmas, John
19. Cook, Roy
20. Cooper, Charlie
21. Creasey, David
22. Crooks, Norman
23. Crosbie, Henry
24. Cummings, Billy
25. Dandridge, Derek
26. Davies, Alan
27. Downs, Ray
28. Embling, Charlie
29. Evans, Evan
30. Fiddler, Ken
31. Flexman, Colin
32. Foster, Reg
33. Gray, Ken
34. Griffin, Cyril
35. Hall, George
36. Hardy, Patrick
37. Hart, Alf
38. Hillman, Gordon
39. Holland, Derek
40. Holmes, Fred
41. Hudson, John
42. Ives, Gerald
43. Jefferies, Les
44. Jones, Maurice
45. Killingrey, Roy
46. Lambert, Bernard
47. Lester, Cyril
48. Little, Ray
49. Marshall, Peter
50. Martin, Doug
51. Marwood, Denis
52. Maslin, Patrick
53. Mason, Colin
54. Matson, Harold
55. McQuade, Bob
56. Meakin, Keith
57. Millar, Donald
58. Morrison, Tommy
59. Murray, Edward
60. Nice, Bernard
61. Nichols, Ivan
62. Paul, James
63. Peake, Gerald
64. Pearson, John
65. Petrie, Alister
66. Phipson, Don
67. Quealy, Glynn
68. Ransome, Terry
69. Reed, Les
70. Reid, Robin
71. Rutherford, Hamish
72. Spradbury, Alan
73. Staples, Billy
74. Symes, Edwin
75. Thrower, John
76. Tylor, Hank
77. Westbury, John
78. White, Graham
79. Wilson, Des
80. Wilson, Vic
81. Windsor, Joe
82. Wrathall, Frank
83. Wright, Steven

Former EMC Personnel (deceased) 2008

1. Adams, Terry
2. Ashcroft, Brian
3. Austin, John
4. Barnes, Gerry
5. Brunton, Clive
6. Carlington, Phil
7. Cole, Norman
8. Costello, Cornelius
9. Davison, Dave.
10. Dobbin, Sqdn.Ldr.
11. Dudley, John
12. Haines, Reg
13. Hippey, Alan
14. Hodgkins, Peter
15. Lindley, Richard
16. Muggleton, Derek
17. New, Tony
18. O'Brien, James
19. Oliver, Geoff
20. Pescador, Frank
21. Pleece, Fred
22. Pogson, Geoff
23. Powell, Tony
24. Reid, Peter
25. Rose, Donald
26. Sadler, George
27. Scott, Geordie Joe
28. Sheppard, John
29. Shore, George
30. Shutt, Sam
31. Thurlow, Fred
32. Stubley, Harry
33. Taylor, Jim
34. Wiltshire, Ray

Former EMC Personnel (not traced) 2008

1. Bacon, John
2. Baker, Gordon
3. Baron, Doug
4. Brecknock Danny,
5. Hutchinson, Derek,
6. Bristow, David
7. Carter, John
8. Catherall, John
9. Cogan, Charles
10. Cox, Peter
11. Curran, Jock
12. Davies/Richards,
13. Stoddart, Robert
14. Fitch, Jock
15. Fox, Len
16. Garcia, Tony
17. Gray, David
18. Grier, John
19. Hollingworth, Peter,
20. Hyland, Nick
21. Mitchell, Peter
22. Morris, Fred
23. Rigby, Tom
24. Scully, Paddy
25. Stevens, Brian
26. Waite, David
27. Wilson, Ray

Additional Information Wanted

If you have any additional information about the Experimental Mobile Column we would be pleased to hear from you. Please contact the curator of the Bourne Hall Museum, Spring Street, Ewell, Surrey KT17 1UF telephone 020 8394 1734